M000297677

# THE
# WAR ON
# CHILDREN

"In 50 years, most of us will be gone and our children will be running the place. Whoever gets to them now will effectively control the future. The war for the hearts and minds of our children is on, and John MacArthur's new book will show you where the strategic battles are being fought and how to engage biblically to take back enemy occupied territory. We must and we will win this war. Our children are depending on us."

—**KIRK CAMERON,** Husband. Father. Actor. Filmmaker.

"The socio-cultural milieu in which we find ourselves today is largely unrecognizable from the world in which I was raised in the mid-twentieth century. This shift is especially apparent in what John MacArthur calls "the war on children," a war that is ultimately an attack on the gospel, the image of God, and the lordship of Jesus Christ. This nefarious war is the product of coalescing cultural, educational, and political forces that jointly contribute to the ongoing disintegration of society. In this helpful corrective, MacArthur applies Scripture to our dire historical moment with relevance, clarity, and faithfulness, encouraging us to saturate the minds of our children, grandchildren, and great-grandchildren in the life-giving power of the gospel. *The War on Children* is biblical, timely, crucial, and refreshing. Read and share!"

—**JOEL R. BEEKE,** Chancellor and Professor of Homiletics & Systematic Theology Puritan Reformed Theological Seminary

"The sanctity of life and the beauty of God's gift of children is increasingly under siege. Dr. R. C. Sproul referred to these recent decades as a period of neo-barbarism. Nowhere today do we see that more than in the way human life is discarded and the image of God defaced. This book from John MacArthur is a timely beacon of biblical truth. Calling Christians to champion a God-centered understanding of children and human dignity, Dr. MacArthur gives us scriptural reasons to guard rising generations fiercely from worldly ideologies. Dr. MacArthur's clarity and conviction remind us of every child's profound value and potential. As we endeavor to serve our King and advance His kingdom faithfully, let us ensure we prioritize and protect the most vulnerable among us."

—**CHRIS LARSON,** President & CEO, Ligonier Ministries

"It's a different world from the one in which we grew up. No longer can we assume that society is bent on keeping children safe and protected. Society is now overrun with people, policies, and programs that are intent on separating young people from Christian principles. Our culture is engaged in a war for our children's souls. In his new book, *The War on Children*, John MacArthur not only gives a wake-up call to parents but offers practical guides to help them safeguard their young ones. This is a book I'll be giving to young parents, seasoned teachers, and anyone whose sphere of influence includes a child."

—**JONI EARECKSON TADA,** Joni and Friends International Disability Center

"Anyone who's been paying attention knows that there is a war on marriage and the family. However, many are oblivious to the fact that there is a war on children. Every developed nation is in the midst of a demographic winter as birthrates plummet. The LGBTQIA2S+ movement is promoting lifestyles that negate the possibility of procreation. Even Christian couples are putting off marriage and childbearing as long as possible, with some foregoing children altogether. Couple this with the onslaught of nihilistic, immoral education, and soul-destroying entertainment, and you've got a recipe for disaster! In *The War on Children*, John MacArthur not only diagnoses the problem boldly and clearly; he also offers a solution. This Christ-exalting book will be a balm to the soul of parents trying to protect their children, and a welcomed encouragement to those who are not sure they want to bring children into this world."

—**VODDIE T. BAUCHAM, JR.,** Dean of Theology, African Christian University

"In *The War on Children*, John MacArthur stands as a watchman on the tower and heralds that a perverse enemy is coming. In fact, the forces of hell are now here. An all-out assault is taking place on the next generation, to brainwash the thinking of children with a devilish ideology that attacks their wellbeing. This timely book sounds a clarion warning that decisive steps must be taken to stem the tide of rampant evil. Every Christian must read this book and be challenged to stop the spread of wickedness that is coming after our children."

—**STEVEN J. LAWSON,** President, OnePassion Ministries
Professor, The Master's Seminary | Teaching Fellow, Ligonier Ministries
Lead Preacher, Trinity Bible Church of Dallas

All Scripture quotations in this book, except those noted otherwise,
are from the New American Standard Bible, © 1960, 1962, 1963,
1968, 1971, 1972, 1973, 1975, 1977, 1988, and 1995 by
The Lockman Foundation, and are used by permission.

Quotations marked LSB are from the Legacy Standard Bible®, (LSB®),
© 2021 by the Lockman Foundation, and are used by permission.

Quotations marked ESV are from THE ENGLISH STANDARD VERSION.
© 2001 by Crossway Bibles, a division of Good News Publishers.

Quotations marked NKJV are from the New King James Version,
© 1984 by Thomas Nelson, Inc.

Quotations marked KJV are from the King James Version of the Bible.

*Wherever words are italicized in Scripture quotations,
the italics have been added for emphasis.*

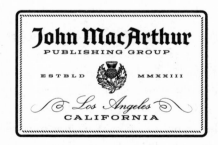

DESIGNED BY WEKREATIVE CO.
ISBN: 978-1-883973-04-9
PRINTED IN CHINA

# THE WAR ON CHILDREN

## PROVIDING REFUGE FOR YOUR CHILDREN IN A HOSTILE WORLD

JOHN MACARTHUR

# CONTENTS

CHAPTER                                                      PAGE

Preface                                                        ix

Introduction                                                   xv


**SECTION 01: SLAUGHTER OF THE INNOCENTS**

1. Shade for Our Children                                      01

2. Whose Children Are They, Anyway?                            15

3. Hampered by the Curse of Sin                               37

4. Children Are a Gift from the Lord                          57

5. The War Is Not Against Flesh and Blood                     83


**SECTION 02: THE KEY BATTLEFRONTS**

6. The Attack on Conception                                   103

7. The Attack on Life                                         125

8. The Attack on the Family                                   143

9. The Attack on Women                                        165

10. The Attack on Men                                         189


Epilogue                                                     209

Endnotes                                                     211

Index of Scripture                                           221

# PREFACE

Most adults can remember the halcyon days when society sought to protect children from harm. Not anymore. Popular culture has turned on the young with an unimaginable barrage of destructive assaults. It is an aggressive campaign being executed with unconscionable malice. The primary goal is to brainwash children through the spread of lies shamelessly intended to obliterate biblical spirituality and morality—and thereby systematically dismantle the foundations of society. Secular social engineers, profane politicians, entertainment moguls, and many business leaders are all in on this sinister strategy. They are determined to raze and totally reshape the culture. In order to accomplish that goal they *must* capture the minds and hearts of the next generation.

Assaults against children are coming from all directions. Propaganda is embedded in children's entertainment, in advertising that targets young people, in the music they listen to, and in their school curriculum. Media produced for children today is practically all infused with ideas that are purposely designed to undermine the biblical values that helped shape Western culture for their ancestors. (If you doubt that, visit any secular bookstore and look at what is being promoted for children to read.) The idea is to indoctrinate future generations with a belief system where good and evil are fundamentally inverted, where gender is not binary but rather a sliding scale with infinite possibilities, where sexual perversions are celebrated, and where God is banished from public discourse.

Christian parents face an especially hard, uphill battle to raise their children "in the discipline and instruction of the Lord" (Ephesians 6:4). Practically every bureaucrat who works in a government agency or public school system is convinced the government knows better than parents how children should be raised and what they should be taught. Furthermore, public schools nowadays are overwhelmingly (and often militantly) anti-Christian.

And the government wants even *more* control over how, when, and what our children are taught. In 2021, President Biden proposed a spending bill with a price tag of $3.5 trillion. Nearly half his proposals had to be cut if the bill had any hope of getting through Congress, but one feature that survived all the cuts— the one major expenditure that proponents of the spending bill boasted about—was a package providing "universal preschool and affordable child care" (at a cost of $400 billion).[1]

One of the frightening implications of this development is that the federal government is now positioned to have the dominant voice in shaping curriculum and educational philosophy for children, starting at age three and continuing through their college years.

It is probably fair to say that in this era where so-called "progressive" policies dominate public policy, *most* government officials are now convinced it is their right, if not their duty, to decide how and what children are taught. In a 2023 ceremony honoring the nation's public school teacher of the year, President Biden said, "There's no such thing as someone else's child. Our nation's children are all our children."[2]

He was echoing a theme liberal politicians have been drumming into the American consciousness for decades. In her 1996 book *It Takes a Village,* Hillary Clinton famously challenged the God-given parental role. She drew her book's title from an oft quoted African proverb, "It takes a village to raise a child." There is of course a germ of truth in the proverb: Kids cannot be properly raised in total isolation, and what they are exposed to in their environment will influence the development of their character. Parents need to make sure they are surrounded with good influences.

But Mrs. Clinton's critics and supporters alike understood that *her* objective in writing the book was to make a not-so-subtle argument against parental rights. She believes the secular state knows better than parents what is in the best interests of today's children. She is therefore convinced that child rearing should be a collectivist enterprise with the government ultimately in charge.

The insinuation that children somehow belong to the government stirred lots of controversy and concern when Mrs. Clinton's book first debuted, but in the decades since, it has gained widespread popularity and overwhelming support among politicians and legislators. In 2022, Vice President Kamala Harris, speaking to a group of mental healthcare professionals, expressed the sentiment this way: "We all believe that when we talk about the children of the community, they are...children of the community."[3]

It's not easy to dismiss that remark as a clumsy, off the cuff verbal fumble—as if it were merely one of Mrs. Harris's trademark giddy tautologies. Slogans and catchphrases like those might even sound perfectly innocuous if our politicians were merely affirming society's duty to guard the innocence of children and keep them safely out of harm's way in matters of moral purity and physical health. But President Biden, Mrs. Harris, and Mrs. Clinton are clearly trying to make the case that the government has an overriding interest in—and therefore ought to have supreme authority over—the moral indoctrination of children.

Indeed, the political party to which all three of these politicians belong has not only advocated, but worse, already enacted legislation specifically designed to diminish or eliminate parents' rights—while granting government agencies increasing authority to decide what values children will be taught. Such high-handed policies are rooted in the belief that parents (especially the religious or conservative ones) are simply incapable of raising their children properly. The conclusion is that it is therefore the prerogative of the government to determine how and what children should be taught.

That notion has become standard policy in public schools, local libraries, the entertainment industry, government agencies, and many large corporations. That's the reason society is now inundated with a flood of people and programs aggressively seeking to indoctrinate young children with values that reflect a radical, secular, and sexually deviant worldview. It explains the push for bizarre new activities targeting children, like graphically explicit sex education for preschoolers, "Drag Queen Story Time," and ubiquitous efforts to involve children in "Gay Pride" celebrations. This is why even the Walt Disney Company has made a concerted effort to insert LGBTQ+ characters into all their children's programming.[4]

Those trends are not likely to be reversed in the near future. Governments do not easily relinquish control once they have seized it. Public schools and government interference in the parenting process will get worse, not better.

Christian parents cannot simply float passively along with the drift of our culture. We need to renew our commitment to wise, careful, attentive, biblical parenting. If you are a parent, you need to recognize that (no matter who you are) your children are not exempt from the ongoing efforts to commandeer their worldview and alienate them from biblical principles.

Above all, realize that this is *war*. It is of course not literally armed combat, but (as we will see in chapter 5) it is even more serious than that. It is a dangerous ideological conflict with eternity at stake. The enemy's aim is to capture your children's hearts and put them in permanent bondage by enslaving them to a sinfully corrupt worldview—a godless, amoral belief system. Your responsibility as parents is to keep them free from that bondage.

You must do that by taking control of what they are taught. Teach them God's Word; train them in righteousness; model righteousness for them; participate in every aspect of their lives; give them wise, biblically-based guidance; and above all, give them your extravagant love.

You cannot isolate your children enough to make sure they are untouched by the world's assaults, but you can shield them from many of the worst influences. Don't leave your children in a public school if they are being bombarded daily with immoral and godless propaganda. Don't enroll them in a private school that is not truly and thoroughly biblical. (A school that is "Christian" in name only may actually be worse than any other option.) Take the lead in teaching your children regardless of what school choice you might make. It is, after all, your duty as a parent to give their lives direction. Train them in the way they should go (Proverbs 22:6), and train them well—especially in matters pertaining to their spiritual growth.

It is to that end that I have written this book. I hope it is a help and encouragement to you as a parent or grandparent seeking to come to your precious children's defense in this brutal war.

# THE SINS OF THE FATHERS

Our children are born with a significant disadvantage: Their parents are sinners. Of course each child starts out fallen, with a sin nature of his or her own. And they are born into a world in which they will endure the impact of the sins of their parents, grandparents, and all the sinful generations that existed before them. They have to live with the cumulative effects of all the wickedness that preceded them. Their world is cursed by sin, and the culture in which they live has been shaped by generations of evildoers.

The Lord describes this reality as part of His righteous judgment. In Exodus 20:5, He admonished the Israelites not to follow the idolatrous ways of the pagan nations, warning them, "I, the LORD your God, am a jealous God, visiting the iniquity of the fathers on the children, on the third and the fourth generations of those who hate Me." Moses notes the same quality of God's judgment as he pleads for God to pardon His people in Numbers 14:18, "The LORD is slow to anger and abundant in lovingkindness, forgiving iniquity and transgression; but He will by no means clear the guilty, visiting the iniquity of the fathers on the children to the third and the fourth generations." The prophet Jeremiah likewise notes that God "repays the iniquity of fathers into the bosom of their children after them" (Jeremiah 32:18).

That doesn't mean God personally punishes children for the specific sins of their parents. Those statements are all qualified by the closing words of Exodus 20:5: "*of those who hate Me.*" It's speaking mainly of people who are participants in the same sins as their fathers and grandfathers. God does not arbitrarily transfer guilt across the generations. The "woke" notion of ethnic or generational guilt is a fallacy. Scripture expressly says, "The person who sins will die. *The son will not bear the punishment for the father's iniquity, nor will the father bear the punishment for the son's iniquity;* the righteousness of the righteous will be upon himself, and the wickedness of the wicked will be upon himself" (Ezekiel 18:20).

Instead, as we will see, Scripture is pointing out that the sins of the fathers collectively create a corrupt culture that children are then born into. This sets children at a severe disadvantage in two ways. One, they will be taught and tempted to perpetuate the sins of their fathers. And two, even if they do not follow in their parents' evil ways, they may bear some of the hurtful *consequences* of a father's or grandfather's sins. For example, children born into families ravaged by drug addiction or alcoholism are forced to deal with the effects of substance abuse from an early age. Others are born into broken homes divided by infidelity and immorality. They have to learn too early about the far-reaching effects of sexual sin. Whatever a parent's sinful proclivities are, his or her children will invariably have to live with damage left in the wake of those sins. In other words, children inherit a world that is shaped and defined by the sins of their parents, and they must navigate their way through the corruption that prior generations have left to them.

Our culture today is the product of centuries of vile and horrific sins. It has been shaped by the wretched desires and wicked intentions of hell-bent hearts. It is a universal reality that each generation passes on to the next a more corrupt world than the one they inherited. In my lifetime alone, the world has rapidly grown more comfortable with sin and more eager to celebrate its pervasive influence. I shudder to think, should the Lord tarry, how future generations will sink further into sin.

That fundamental axiom is acknowledged throughout history, even in ancient literature. A fragment from Euripides' ancient Greek tragedy *Phrixus* (written four hundred years before Christ) includes this line: "The gods visit the sins of the fathers on the children." In *Odes*, a four-volume work of Latin poetry, the Roman poet Horace (65–8 BC) wrote, "For the sins of the fathers you, though guiltless, must suffer" (3.6.1). And in *The Merchant of Venice*, Shakespeare opened scene five of act three with the merchant stating the same axiom: "Yes, truly; for, look you, the sins of the fathers are to be laid upon the children."

But what disturbs me most about the twenty-first-century world—what grieves my heart more than anything else—is the way our media, educational institutions, and other influencers in our culture (including government officials and government agencies) are waging war on children.

Today we are not merely contending with the normal, accumulated evil of past generations. We're also living in a culture that has specifically targeted children for destruction. Every day, on a multitude of battlefronts, Satan is deploying weapons of mass corruption against our children. Modern culture has been systematically designed with an agenda that is aggressively anti-God, anti-Christ, and anti-Scripture, intended to corrupt and consume young, impressionable hearts and minds. Preoccupied, foolish parents offer little resistance.

Through the genocide of abortion, children are under fire from this world before they even leave the womb. With the breakdown of the family and the perversion of God's design for marriage, the home offers little, if any, protection from the world's attacks. Schoolteachers, politicians, and tech oligarchs all promote their own destructive ideologies and worldviews, indoctrinating young minds as early as possible. Entertainers and media moguls routinely pump out content designed to deceive and degenerate—and our children are their principle targets.

God's people need to be aware of the specific threats this world poses to our children. We need to understand the enemy's battle plan and be ready to spot where the next assault is coming from. And we need to prepare our children for the attacks they will inevitably face from a culture intent on their destruction.

This world has declared war on our children. Are you ready to fight?

# SLAUGHTER OF THE INNOCENTS

# CHAPTER ONE

# SHADE FOR OUR CHILDREN

One of the greatest blessings I have in my life is the fact that our four children are faithful followers of Christ. That is largely owing to my wife, Patricia, for her unwavering commitment to Christ and the righteous example she has set for our children. They didn't just have a preacher as a father; they had a role model in their mother.

In addition to Patricia's influence, many friends and saints in our church have played a significant role in shaping the lives of my children, grandchildren, and even great-grandchildren. The impact of Grace Community Church has reinforced the values and convictions they grew up learning. I am profoundly grateful for this.

As parents, grandparents, and now great-grandparents, we have navigated the challenges of the world and have seen the hand of the Lord and His grace at work. It is encouraging to know that despite the difficulties presented by our culture, Christian parenting—rooted in the Word of God and godly living within a faithful church community—is God's design for raising the next generation to love and follow Jesus. That goal is achievable, and although cultural trends may appear to place insurmountable obstacles in the way of biblical parenting, all the strategies employed by the evil one to corrupt our children can be overcome by the power of God when we faithfully align our lives and families with His revealed will.

A Chinese proverb wisely states, "One generation plants the trees, and the next generation enjoys the shade." That sums up the crucial role each generation should play in shielding our children from evil influences and thus securing a better future for them. It is a reminder for all of us to recognize our duty in shaping the character of the children God has given us.

Today we face formidable challenges. Among all the distressing issues and false ideologies that are contributing to the moral and spiritual breakdown of our culture, none is more fiercely destructive, and none threatens to do more sinister, long-term damage than the war on children. Virtually every aspect of our culture is being weaponized to harm and corrupt children systematically. The destruction starts before birth with murder in the womb. The staggering number of abortions since Roe v. Wade in the 1970s, totaling 62.5 million, is a heartbreaking statistic.[5]

Beyond even that, we are seeing the deliberate breakdown of the traditional family structure. A child's chances of even being born to a married couple now hover around 50/50. Then come the powerful and relentless cultural pressures and influences. Public schools expose children to anti-God, anti-Christ, and anti-biblical ideologies. Our country's leaders enact laws that protect those who are devastating children by demanding sexual freedom, by celebrating homosexuality, by promoting transgenderism, and by seeking to normalize those concepts while punishing anyone who opposes them. False narratives like systemic racism dominate universities and even churches. Entertainment industries, social media, and big tech promote content that harms children.

Our kids are under crafty assaults from the forces of evil, and they are defenseless. Moreover, our society and culture seem determined to enable those responsible for this destruction to continue unchecked. Even some parents deliberately subject their children to evils ranging from gender confusion to human trafficking.

Children are specifically targeted, while the government seeks only to protect the perpetrators. The U.S. President has expressed his intent to provide government funded education from the age of three to twenty. This paints a grim picture, because government schools nationwide have already made clear that they are determined to indoctrinate elementary schoolchildren with beliefs and worldviews that are overtly anti-Christian, immoral, and patently inappropriate for children so young. Now education officials in the government want access to even younger toddlers, to control what the next generation will be taught from the time they begin to socialize, well into adulthood. Government-run school officials are convinced that managing a child's mind is the prerogative of Caesar, not Christ. From leading politicians, bureaucrats, teachers, race hustlers, pornographers, media figures, tech giants, and even some medical professionals, children, the most vulnerable among us, face relentless assault. This is an all-out war on children.

It is important to acknowledge that all children, even in the best of circumstances, face major spiritual challenges—not only because they are born to sinful parents, but also because they themselves are sinful. They enter the world fallen, inheriting the nature and effects of their parents' sins. Exodus 20:5 is literally embedded in the Ten Commandments. It is a comment on the second commandment, highlighting the evil and the far-reaching dangers of idolatry. This is the first of several texts in Scripture where we are told that God visits the iniquity of the parents down on the children to the third and fourth generations. Exodus 34:7, Numbers 14:18, and Deuteronomy 5:9 all use the same terminology to repeat the warning that the sins of the fathers are a major impediment to the spiritual health of children. In Jeremiah 32:17–18 the same truth is reiterated, even in the context of praise to God for His power and His mercy: "Ah Lord GOD! Behold, You have made the heavens and the earth by Your great power and by Your outstretched arm! Nothing is too difficult for You, who shows lovingkindness to thousands, *but repays the iniquity of fathers into the bosom of their children after them.*" Jeremiah 31:29 restates the same principle in these words: "The fathers have eaten sour grapes, and the children's teeth are set on edge."

As we noted in the introduction, however, God does not arbitrarily or indiscriminately punish children for their parents' sins. Instead, the sins of a generation collectively shape the culture that subsequent generations have to endure. This is an obvious reality. Whatever is true of one generation will inevitably affect the next. All children are born sinful and are exposed to the sin and corruption passed down from previous generations.

In Deuteronomy 5, as the Israelites stood on the cusp of the Promised Land—ready to receive the inheritance they had long ago been promised—the Lord warned them of the generational effects of their sin.

I am the LORD your God who brought you out of the land of Egypt, out of the house of slavery.

You shall have no other gods before Me.

You shall not make for yourself an idol, or any likeness of what is in heaven above or on the earth beneath or in the water under the earth. You shall not worship them or serve them; for I, the LORD your God, am a jealous God, visiting the iniquity of the fathers on the children, and on the third and the fourth generations of those who hate Me. (Deuteronomy 5:6–9)

Again, the message is clear: Your sin has consequences for your children. But there is hope. In verse 10 the Lord continues, "But [I show] lovingkindness to thousands, to those who love Me and keep My commandments." God has graciously provided a way for children to escape the compounded corruption of past generations' sin. Because God has provided a way of redemption, those who love Him and keep His commandments—those whose trust is truly in the Lord—can survive and (by God's grace) even be lifted above both their own fallenness and the wicked world into which they were born.

In that regard, Deuteronomy presents us with an instructive illustration. The Israelites were ready and eager to enter Canaan. It was the Promised Land, but it was a pagan land. It contained no godly influences whatsoever—no one who worshiped the true and living God. During Israel's centuries in Egyptian captivity, the land had been occupied by tribes of idol worshipers, engaging in the worst kinds of paganism. It was a land fully engulfed in satanic influences and practices.

Deuteronomy 6 recounts the instructions God gave to His people through Moses as they prepared to enter Canaan.

> Now this is the commandment, the statutes and the judgments
> which the LORD your God has commanded me to teach you,
> that you might do them in the land where you are going over
> to possess it, so that you and your son and your grandson
> might fear the LORD your God, to keep all His statutes and His
> commandments which I command you, all the days of your
> life, and that your days may be prolonged. (vv. 1–2)

God is clear that each generation has a responsibility to teach
their children and grandchildren. Specifically, God's people are
responsible to teach their offspring to fear Him and live faithfully
according to His Word. It is our duty as believers to train those
who come after us to love, worship, and obey the Lord. Just as we
have submitted our lives to Him, we must teach our offspring to
do the same.

Verse 3 continues, "O Israel, you should listen and be careful
to do it, that it may be well with you and that you may multiply
greatly, just as the LORD, the God of your fathers, has promised
you, in a land flowing with milk and honey." In other words, do
everything the Lord commands you to do. Fear and obey Him
all your life, so that you can pass that godly example on to your
children and grandchildren, that they might also enjoy the full
blessings of a life submitted to Him.

God is saying that if you want a prosperous life, if you want
to pass on righteousness to subsequent generations, you must
be faithful. And faithfulness starts with your own heart. Verse 4
is the Shema, Old Testament Israel's monotheistic, foundational
confession of faith. Moses exhorted the people, "Hear, O Israel!
The LORD is our God, the LORD is one! You shall love the LORD
your God with all your heart and with all your soul and with all
your might. These words, which I am commanding you today,
shall be on your heart" (vv. 4–6). You must love God alone, with

your entire being. Furthermore, love and obedience to God are to be deeply ingrained from generation to generation.

Israel was heading into enemy territory, where countless idols dominated every aspect of life and posed significant temptations to God's people. The pagan ritual feasts and orgies would have enticed the Israelites' flesh, and we know the sad history of their repeated spiritual compromise.

The brand of idolatry that dominates our world today does not look exactly like Canaanite religion, but it is no less sinister. And make no mistake: It is still idolatry, and everything about it is rooted in paganism (anti-biblical religious beliefs). The world around us is still filled with temptations constantly appealing to our flesh. Enticements to sin are ubiquitous in today's world, and they are constantly pushed at us via the Internet and other media. We need to remember that whether we withstand those temptations and hold fast to God or fail to do so, our choices bear repercussions not only in our lives but for the generations that follow.

The Lord's instructions become more specific in verse 7. Regarding His commandments, He says, "You shall teach them diligently to your sons and shall talk of them when you sit in your house and when you walk by the way and when you lie down and when you rise up." The constant theme of life is to be the Word of God. From dawn to dusk, God's truth must dominate your family's life and conversation. The goal is always the same—namely, obedience to the law of God, with an all-encompassing love for Him.

That point is reinforced in verses 8 and 9, "You shall bind them as a sign on your hand and they shall be as frontals on your forehead. You shall write them on the doorposts of your house and on your gates." This signifies the importance of aligning your actions with God's law and keeping your mind focused on Him and His commandments. The most fastidious orthodox Jews interpreted this text with strict literalism. They wore phylacteries—small boxes containing written copies of the Shema. But the command in this verse is not about external symbols (as if there were some mystical or magical value in a physical printout of the text). The command is a reminder that our hands should operate in response to the law of God; that our minds should be concentrating on His Word at all times; and that whether we are coming or going, His truth should direct and animate our thoughts and our conduct. Put simply, *love for God and submission to His Word should control us all the time, everywhere, in everything we think, say, or do.*

In verse 9, Scripture adds, "You shall write them on the doorposts of your house and on your gates." Again, the point of this command is that God's Word should permeate every aspect of your life, whether you are inside or outside the home. Hang a mezuzah on your doorpost, or literally engrave a verse of Scripture on the door if you like, but don't imagine that this alone fulfills this command. Such practices are symbolic. They simply represent the need for God's Word to be the authority by which we live, and that we must submit to God's truth constantly, consistently, and unconditionally—"when you sit in your house and when you walk by the way and when you lie down and when you rise up" (v. 7).

The Lord then directs their attention to the rich blessings they were about to receive. "Then it shall come about when the LORD your God brings you into the land which He swore to your fathers, Abraham, Isaac and Jacob, to give you, great and splendid cities which you did not build, and houses full of all good things which you did not fill, and hewn cisterns which you did not dig, vineyards and olive trees which you did not plant, and you eat and are satisfied" (vv. 10–11). Even while Israel was in captivity, God had been preparing the land for His people through the work of the pagan civilizations He was about to judge.

But the good news of their forthcoming inheritance came with a stark warning:

> Watch yourself, that you do not forget the LORD who brought you from the land of Egypt, out of the house of slavery. You shall fear only the LORD your God; and you shall worship Him and swear by His name. You shall not follow other gods, any of the gods of the peoples who surround you, for the LORD your God in the midst of you is a jealous God; otherwise the anger of the LORD your God will be kindled against you, and He will wipe you off the face of the earth. (vv. 12–15)

Even in prosperity, it is vital to maintain reverence for God. He alone deserves worship and allegiance, even if it sets us against the rest of the world. Our God is a jealous God. He will not be mocked. He won't share the affections of His people with anyone or anything. That was not news to the Israelites—they had received a similar warning, recorded just two chapters earlier.

> The LORD your God is a consuming fire, a jealous God.
>
> When you become the father of children and children's children and have remained long in the land, and act corruptly, and make an idol in the form of anything, and do that which is evil in the sight of the LORD your God so as to provoke Him to anger, I call heaven and earth to witness against you today, that you will surely perish quickly from the land where you are going over the Jordan to possess it. You shall not live long on it, but will be utterly destroyed. The LORD will scatter you among the peoples, and you will be left few in number among

the nations where the LORD drives you. There you will serve gods, the work of man's hands, wood and stone, which neither see nor hear nor eat nor smell. (Deuteronomy 4:24–28)

Thus God promises to deal severely with those who commit spiritual infidelity and those who fail to faithfully shepherd subsequent generations in the nurture and admonition of the Lord. He says He will wipe them off the face of the earth.

You would think a dire warning like that would stick with the people who received it. But it wasn't long before Israel was committing the very sins the Lord had warned against, inviting His wrath and judgment. The book of Judges describes the end of Joshua's life, and how Israel quickly fell away from following God.

When Joshua had dismissed the people, the sons of Israel went each to his inheritance to possess the land. The people served the LORD all the days of Joshua, and all the days of the elders who survived Joshua, who had seen all the great work of the LORD which He had done for Israel. Then Joshua the son of Nun, the servant of the LORD, died at the age of one hundred and ten.... All that generation also were gathered to their fathers; and there arose another generation after them who did not know the LORD, nor yet the work which He had done for Israel. (Judges 2:6–8, 10)

In just one generation, Israel turned away from God. In just one generation, they forgot who He is and all He had done for them. What a disaster to not pass on the rich history of His covenant promises and His faithful provision! What a catastrophe not to impart that spiritual truth and wisdom to the next generation of God's covenant people!

The generation that had come with Joshua into the Promised Land remained faithful, having witnessed all the miraculous events of the Exodus, the wilderness journey, God's provision of food and protection, the conquest of Canaan, and the fall of Jericho. Scripture tells us, "The people served the LORD all the days of Joshua, and all the days of the elders who survived Joshua, who had seen all the great work of the LORD which He had done for Israel" (Judges 2:7). Their faithfulness was commendable.

However, verse 8 marks the passing of Joshua, who died at the age of 110. He was buried on the property he inherited in Timnath-heres, in the hill country of Ephraim, north of Mount Gaash. Verse 10 also records the passing of that faithful generation, who joined their ancestors.

But tragically, the new generation that emerged did not know the Lord or the great works He had done for Israel. Consider what Israel *should* have known about God from the earliest days of Old Testament history. They should have known about His creative work, the rebellion of Adam and Eve, and God's faithfulness to them in spite of their sin. They should have known about the speedy corruption of the world, culminating in God's judgment through the Flood, and His faithfulness to Noah and his family—they should have been reminded of it every time they saw a rainbow. They should have known about God's promises to their father Abraham, and how those promises were fulfilled in the lives of Isaac and Jacob. They certainly should have known about God's miraculous work through Moses to deliver His people out of Egypt, through the wilderness, and into the land they inhabited. How could such a unique heritage of unmatched blessing be lost in the span of just one generation?

In spite of Israel's failure to teach their children to love and follow God, He kept His promises to them—in this case, promises of judgment.

That generation's failure to honor God's faithfulness to their parents proved unthinkably disastrous. The younger generation fell into apostasy and divine judgment: "Then the sons of Israel did evil in the sight of the LORD and served the Baals, and they forsook the LORD, the God of their fathers...thus they provoked the LORD to anger" (vv. 11–12). They turned away from the Lord who had brought them out of Egypt! Worse yet, "They forsook the LORD and served Baal and the Ashtaroth" (v. 13). The parents' failure to instruct their children led to predictable outcomes—evil actions, culminating in the worship of other gods, putting the whole nation under God's judgment. It stands as a monumental failure for that generation of otherwise faithful parents.

A similar apostasy is at work today, drawing the sons and daughters of Christians away from their parents' faith. The world clamors for our children's acquiescence to amoral values and unbiblical beliefs. Our culture is teeming with temptations. The airwaves and Internet are rife with influencers who despise the truth of Scripture and whose goal is to indoctrinate the next generation. Over the past half-century their efforts have fundamentally transformed American culture. The moral fabric of our culture has already unraveled—and this long, indefatigable campaign to corrupt the minds and moral values of young children is one of the most destructive forces at the root of the problem. Biblical faith, once a major force in Western culture, is now deemed a fringe belief system. It is deliberately undermined, mocked, and opposed at almost every level, from public school curriculum to the music and entertainment that is being pushed at our children.

Tireless efforts to eliminate childlike innocence are now underway at almost every level of society. Moral values are methodically turned upside down—often by redefinition. The virtues and values on which Western society was built are casually rejected as too old-fashioned simply because that's what our parents' and grandparents' generations believed. Meanwhile, radical sexual perversions are aggressively marketed as "progressive" (no matter how destructive they might be to society's moral order). Things that ought to be universally recognized as true are routinely questioned.

Even essential, axiomatic truths are peremptorily denied in the push to make room for the new moral disorder. Something as basic and obvious as the essential biological difference between male and female is now considered immaterial in the determination of a child's gender. The classification of a child's sex on the birth certificate is popularly regarded as merely provisional. It is just a category "assigned at birth" (as if randomly) by an obstetrician—and what does he know about gender?

Anyone who pays attention can easily see that popular culture no longer values the innocence of childhood. Actually, that is an understatement. Childhood itself is under fierce assault on multiple fronts. Forces in government, education, entertainment, and the media are waging an aggressive campaign to reprogram how our children think about virtue, gender, and basic human decency. At the same time, they are overtly attacking timeless biblical standards and systematically dismantling the moral foundations of civilized culture.

This siege is happening virtually everywhere in the Western world. Defenseless children are the primary victims of societies that have been morally bankrupted by lies, godlessness, sexual immorality, divorce, feminism, abortion, pornography, the dismantling of manhood and the place of fathers, the death of family values, and a vast web of interconnected evil influences. All these forces, with strong support from the government, media, big businesses, and the entertainment industry are waging an open and successful propaganda campaign at children from preschool to college, indoctrinating them with a sinister worldview that spurns essential biblical principles and, ultimately, truth itself.

Believers must understand that we live in hostile territory, surrounded by satanic ideologies designed to lead hearts away from God and the truth of His Word. Christian parents today face an extreme challenge, in many ways far more difficult than most of our immediate ancestors ever had to contend with. Ironically, some of the things that supposedly make our lives more convenient—television, the Internet, text messaging, and smart phones—add to the difficulties we face in trying to protect our children from this world's assaults.

"So then let us not sleep as others do, but let us be alert and sober" (1 Thessalonians 5:6). While there's nothing we can do to guarantee a child's salvation, we must do everything we can to protect the children God entrusts to us from the confusing, corrupting, and degrading influences of a perversely wicked world.

# CHAPTER TWO

# WHOSE CHILDREN ARE THEY, ANYWAY?

The war on children has been underway for several decades, but it has lately become so overt and aggressive that it is impossible to ignore. Children are now being openly groomed en masse by people with debauched moral values and perverted sexual preferences. You see clear evidence of this in the epidemic of "Drag Queen Story Time" sessions sponsored by schools, libraries, and bookstores across America. You see it in public school districts that view protective parents as adversarial intruders who have no right to protect their own children from the predators who seduce them into sinful, life-destroying corruptions. You see it in countless videos posted on the Internet by teachers parading their own deviant behavior and ideology in efforts to debauch children. You see it in the medical community's sinister greed, marketing transgender surgeries for children. The macabre and irreversible abuse and mutilation of children's minds and bodies are deceptively referred to as "gender-affirming care" or "transgender care."

The entire moral fabric of society has been unraveled and is being rearranged so that what used to be deemed immorality is now celebrated and what used to be seen as virtuous is now scorned. Indeed, the powers that be at almost every level of our society demand that everyone must celebrate immorality and perversion. This radical reversal of values is openly promoted in the curriculum used by government-funded school systems. It dominates the music industry's offerings for young people. It is further diffused through children's entertainment—animated features, television programming, and even picture books. Some of the recommended reading in local libraries features cartoon images graphically showing children how to indulge in deviant sexual activities. School boards across the country have defended the inclusion of such resources in their libraries. The bottom-line design of the whole project is to mold young minds to believe it is normal, healthy, and good to celebrate twisted things, while telling them that the biblical values underlying most of Western culture are responsible for virtually every evil we face.

What I am describing is a decades-long, full-scale war against children. It has been underway and steadily escalating for more than a half-century. It has already had a significant deleterious effect on several generations of people who are now adults. Young people now in their twenties and thirties belong to the first generation that seems thoroughly indoctrinated.

There are exceptions, of course, but the typical twenty-something today has been trained to embrace the idea of entitlement while spurning the concept of responsibility. They have been taught that honor, innocence, and moral purity are abnormal, but promiscuity and perversion are to be embraced, flaunted, and even celebrated in debauched public exhibitions with "Pride." Young people have been force-fed a value system that deliberately undermines the God-ordained role of parents and family while magnifying the importance of government and community in shaping a young person's moral convictions and behavioral boundaries. Kids are now being aggressively groomed and coached on such matters beginning in nursery school. Christianity and common sense have been cast aside, and majority opinion has already shifted against any return to moral sanity.

The predictable result of all this? It has not only shattered families; it has shredded the fabric of society as well. Crime, homelessness, drug abuse, suicide, divorce, and a host of other societal ills are rooted in this push to capture the minds and hearts of children. It is no exaggeration to say that it is a war—and a fierce one. It is precisely the kind of warfare described in 2 Corinthians 10:3–5:

> Though we walk in the flesh, we do not war according to the flesh, for the weapons of our warfare are not of the flesh, but divinely powerful for the destruction of fortresses. We are destroying speculations and every lofty thing raised up against the knowledge of God, and we are taking every thought captive to the obedience of Christ.

In other words, this is an ideological war, where our duty as Christians is to expose lies with the truth, answer evil ideas with righteous ones, and overthrow wicked false opinions with a biblical worldview.

It is particularly important that we fight this war faithfully on behalf of our children, because in reality they are not merely our children. Children belong to God in a unique and vital sense. That is true of all children.

Children are not property of the government, the community at large, the village council, the department of education, the local school district, or some elite class of "experts." Every child is a unique treasure created by God for His own sovereign purpose. And while He graciously places children in *their parents'* care and custody, He does not hand them over as if they were chattel. Parents are not entitled owners; they are uniquely accountable to God as stewards and caretakers of the children He has given them. The prophet Isaiah acknowledged this when he spoke of his own two sons as "the children whom the LORD has given me" (Isaiah 8:18). The New Testament reveals that there is a prophetic sense in that expression; it is how Christ views those whom He redeems (Hebrews 2:13). There's a lesson for all parents implied in that prophetic connection—namely, that we should safeguard and cherish our children the way Christ does those whom He redeems.

God's own paternal interest and His tender mercies extend in a particular way to children who are too young to make independent moral choices for themselves (Jonah 4:11; Matthew 19:13–14). We will shortly be looking closely at His angry condemnation of people who sacrifice their infants or toddlers to pagan idols. But first of all, note that in this context, the Lord pointedly refers to these little ones as "*My* children" (Ezekiel 16:21). They belong to Him in a special sense.

So parenting is a stewardship, a privilege, and a sweet gift from the generous hand of a benevolent God. Parenting is obviously a weighty responsibility, but a child is a precious blessing and living proof of God's grace, not a mere burden or inconvenience. "Like arrows in the hand of a warrior, so are the children of one's youth. How blessed is the man whose quiver is full of them" (Psalm 127:4–5).

In the previous chapter, we noted how the generation after Joshua "forsook the LORD and served Baal and the Ashtaroth"

(Judges 2:13). Baal and the Ashtaroth were ancient deities worshiped by pagan cultures. Baal was often referred to as the "lord of heaven," supposedly the son of a god named El, who was associated with rain, storms, and fertility. He was worshiped with lewd dances. He was as morally bankrupt as all the Canaanite deities. "Worship" of him involved acts of fornication with sacred prostitutes, both men and women.

Ashtaroth, described as Baal's sister wife, was believed to be the goddess of sex and war. She was associated with sacred prostitution, and yet she was sometimes referred to as a holy virgin. The Israelites fell into gross idolatry in a single generation.

Judges 2:14–15 says,

> The anger of the LORD burned against Israel, and He gave them into the hands of plunderers who plundered them; and He sold them into the hands of their enemies around them, so that they could no longer stand before their enemies. Wherever they went, the hand of the LORD was against them for evil, as the LORD had spoken and as the LORD had sworn to them, so that they were severely distressed.

When one generation fails to pass on righteous instruction to the next, God's judgment is inevitable.

Verses 16 and 17 say God "raised up judges." It was not a monarchy; these weren't national rulers. They were simply deliverers whom God raised up at different points to protect the people of Israel from complete oblivion.

> Then the LORD raised up judges who delivered them from the hands of those who plundered them. Yet they did not listen to their judges, for they played the harlot after other gods and bowed themselves down to them. They turned aside quickly

from the way in which their fathers had walked in obeying the commandments of the LORD; they did not do as their fathers.

This pattern persisted through several generations. The rest of the book of Judges goes on to chronicle Israel's tragic cycle of sin, rebellion, judgment, repentance, and more sin over the next three hundred years. The iniquity escalated across all those generations. The nation collectively seemed to abandon any concern for righteousness, and individuals pursued their own desires without restraint or compunction. It all culminates in the devastating testimony recorded in Judges 21:25, "In those days there was no king in Israel; everyone did what was right in his own eyes."

That was exactly contrary to what God had commanded through Moses in Deuteronomy 12:8: "You shall not do at all what we are doing here today, *every man doing whatever is right in his own eyes*." Unfortunately, they disregarded the Lord's admonition and continued relentlessly down the wrong path for three centuries, forsaking the one true God and failing to transmit the knowledge of God to subsequent generations. This failure to raise children in the nurture and admonition of the Lord (and in the fear of God) led to a disastrous situation spanning multiple generations. It meant that each new generation was born into an increasingly sinful and corrupt culture, inviting more divine judgment.

But it's remarkable that it took just one generation for Israel to fall away from God. The subsequent centuries of rebellion deepened the divide to the point that the nation was marked by utter lawlessness and freewheeling wickedness. One generation of parents and grandparents failed to erect doctrinal guardrails, and the whole nation careened off into spiritual disaster for centuries.

Moses had also warned that if the Israelites failed to pass on their knowledge of God and their love for Him, the chief victims of that oversight would be the children. He told them, "Be careful to listen to all these words which I command you, so that it may be well with you and your sons after you forever" (Deuteronomy 12:28). They received that charge before they ever entered the Promised Land. The welfare of their own little ones was what was at stake if they did not remain faithful.

The warning continued, and Moses got very explicit:

> When the LORD your God cuts off before you the nations which you are going in to dispossess, and you dispossess them and dwell in their land, beware that you are not ensnared to follow them, after they are destroyed before you, and that you do not inquire after their gods, saying, "How do these nations serve their gods, that I also may do likewise?" You shall not behave thus toward the LORD your God, for every abominable act which the LORD hates they have done for their gods... (Deuteronomy 12:29–31)

Here's how bad it got: *"They even burn their sons and daughters in the fire to their gods"* (v. 31).

Not only were Canaanite children fallen and prone to sin by nature (like their parents and everyone else), but they were also living in a depraved culture shaped by generations of corruption and idolatry. Worst of all, parents in that culture went even further by murdering their children as sacrifices offered to idols.

Historians and archaeologists studying the ancient world are still discovering proofs of just how pervasive this practice became throughout the world in the Old Testament era. The city of Carthage (situated on the north coast of Africa, where Tunis, Tunisia, is located today) was home to the most cruel, ghastly form of child sacrifice ever practiced.[6] The city had been founded as a Phoenician maritime settlement nearly a millennium before the time of Christ, and it quickly grew into a large and powerful city. Carthage was a major center of world trade and commerce from the ninth century BC until it was conquered by Rome in the second century AD. Their predilection for child sacrifice was known throughout the world.

The Phoenicians who founded Carthage were a culture of seafaring traders who had emerged from among the Canaanites. Phoenician influence stretched from the Canaanite region of Tyre and Sidon (on the Mediterranean coast directly north of Israel) to Carthage and beyond, virtually blanketing the Mediterranean world.

In all likelihood, the sinister practice of child sacrifice had been brought to Carthage from the Phoenician home base in Canaan, because we know from Scripture that the sacrifice of babies and small children had been a staple of the pagan religions that dominated the Promised Land before the time of Joshua. So the style of child sacrifice that was practiced in ancient Carthage gives us an indication of what child sacrifice in the Old Testament probably looked like.

Researchers from Oxford University have shown that child sacrifice was practiced in Carthage.[7] The Carthaginians had made a massive bronze statue with a human body and the head of a bull. The idol's arms were outstretched as if to receive an infant, but the arms were positioned slightly downward. The lower part of the metallic structure—the lap of the idol—housed a furnace. Heated to a super-high temperature, it was used to incinerate children. Live babies would be placed in the idol's arms, and as heat from the fire below caused the child to curl up, the victim would fall from the arms of the bronze idol, through an opening in the figure's lap, directly into the white-hot furnace.

Countless children were willingly sacrificed in this manner by their own parents. When parents ran out of children, they would resort to buying poor children and paying their destitute parents for the child to be used as a sacrifice. This was the abhorrent practice in a godless culture. One historian says, "The sound of complaint was drowned in the din of flutes and kettledrums. Mothers, according to Plutarch, stood by without tears or sobs; if they wept or sobbed they lost the honour of the act, and their children were sacrificed notwithstanding."[8]

That perfectly echoes a description of Carthaginian child sacrifice that dates as far back as Diodorus of Sicily (an ancient historian from the first century BC). He says, "There was in [Carthage] a bronze image...extending its hands, palms up and sloping toward the ground, so that each of the children when placed thereon rolled down and fell into a sort of gaping pit filled with fire."[9]

Diodorus says the idol represented a fierce, bloodthirsty deity named "Cronus." Cronus was a Greek Titan known for eating his own children. The Romans identified him with their god Saturn. Scholars believe he was also the model for several notorious Canaanite gods, including Baal and Molech.

Molech is the sinister deity worshiped by the Ammonite tribe. He is called "Molech the detestable idol of the sons of Ammon" (1 Kings 11:7). He is also known as "Moloch" (Acts 7:43) and "Milcom" (2 Kings 23:13). The Moabites worshiped a similar deity under the name "Chemosh" (1 Kings 11:7). Molech's devotees believed he could be appeased only by the sacrifice of young children.

We don't know precisely how pagan religious ceremonies were carried out in the Canaanite and Ammonite cultures of the Old Testament. Scripture gives no detailed description. But because of the close cultural connections between Carthage and Canaan, illustrations of Molech are usually modeled on the actual idol that was used for child sacrifice in Carthage.

The only fact Scripture records about the evil ritual is that fire was the means by which children were offered to the idol. In any case, the Bible makes it clear that an abominable form of child sacrifice was common among the pagans, and the practice later became a perpetual snare during times of apostasy in ancient Israel, so that even among the Israelites, children were immolated as offerings to pagan gods. Scripture repeatedly condemns parents who "made their sons and their daughters pass through the fire" (2 Kings 17:17). That same expression is used at least a dozen times in the Old Testament. No matter how you conceive it, the idea is savage and horrific—a monstrous violation of the most basic instincts of natural human affection.

Such practices were, of course, strictly forbidden by God. In Deuteronomy 18:9–10 He told the Israelites: "When you enter the land which the LORD your God gives you, you shall not learn to imitate the detestable things of those nations. There shall not be found among you anyone who makes his son or his daughter pass through the fire." The first mention of Molech worship in the Bible comes from Moses's hand as well, when he reiterates the prohibition against the horror of child sacrifice: "You shall not give any of your offspring to offer them to Molech, nor shall you profane the name of your God; I am the LORD" (Leviticus 18:21).

Unconscionably, however, when the Israelites eventually settled in the land, they *did* offer some of their children to the idol flames. This of course was one of the grossest evils that apostates and unbelievers in the Old Testament could possibly have fallen into—and it happened repeatedly.

Sometime after the Jewish kingdom divided in the wake of Solomon's death, child sacrifice became common enough that a specific location on the outskirts of Jerusalem was devoted to Molech worship. It was a place known as Tophet, meaning "the place of burning." The Lord spoke of it through the prophet Jeremiah: "They have built the high places of Topheth, which is in the valley of the son of Hinnom, to burn their sons and their daughters in the fire, which I did not command, and it did not come into My mind" (Jeremiah 7:31).

The prophet Ezekiel sheds further light on this issue. Nearly a thousand years after the time of Moses, God's indictment of the practice was as clear and emphatic as ever. In Ezekiel 16:20–21, He rebukes them: "You took your sons and daughters *whom you had borne to Me* and sacrificed them to idols to be devoured. Were your harlotries so small a matter? You slaughtered *My children* and offered them up to idols by causing them to pass through the fire."

The implication is clear. Children, in the truest sense, belong to the Lord Himself. A few verses later, referring to the sexual immorality that characterized pagan religious practices, God through the prophet declares,

> Because your lewdness was poured out and your nakedness uncovered through your harlotries with your lovers and with all your detestable idols, and because of the blood of your sons which you gave to idols, therefore, behold, I will gather all your lovers with whom you took pleasure, even all those whom you loved and all those whom you hated. So I will gather them against you from every direction and expose your nakedness to them that they may see all your nakedness. Thus I will judge you like women who commit adultery or shed blood are judged; and I will bring on you the blood of wrath and jealousy. (Ezekiel 16:36–38)

Thus God pronounced judgment on them for their failure to protect and teach their children as He had commanded. The Israelites had engaged in the very acts that God explicitly warned them against! It is unimaginable that they would go to such extremes as to offer their own children in sacrificial fires.

But the issue of child sacrifice is a theme that runs through Old Testament history. Ezekiel 20:30–31 says, "Thus says the Lord GOD, 'Will you defile yourselves after the manner of your fathers and play the harlot after their detestable things? When you offer your gifts, when you cause your sons to pass through the fire, you are defiling yourselves with all your idols to this day. And shall I be inquired of by you, O house of Israel? As I live,' declares the Lord GOD, 'I will not be inquired of by you.'"

Ezekiel 23:37 is a stern indictment: "They have committed adultery, and blood is on their hands. Thus they have committed adultery with their idols and even caused their sons, whom they bore to Me, to pass through the fire to them as food." In other words, they fed God's children to Satan's false gods! Then they tried to paper over their evil idolatry with a show of piety to the true God. But so blinded were they to both God's holiness and their own wickedness that their pretense of worshiping the Lord became corrupted with the same evils as their idol worship.

More shocking yet, verse 39 says, "When they had slaughtered their children for their idols, they entered My sanctuary on the same day to profane it; and lo, thus they did within My house." In other words, they went from sacrificing their children at idol temples to joining the public, corporate worship in the house of Israel's God! Don't—*please don't*—blaspheme God by pretending to worship Him on the Sabbath if you just offered your children to a god as human sacrifice.

Forsaking the true God and His worship and obedience was and is a multigenerational disaster, a tragedy of massive proportions that invites the wrath of God.

It is amazing and appalling to see how many cultures throughout history have engaged in child sacrifice—and pretended that this was a religious sacrament. There is no hemisphere on earth where children have not been ceremoniously sacrificed. The practice was as common in Aztec and Incan idolatry as it was with the Canaanites and Phoenicians. Archaeological evidence abounds to show that child sacrifice was more the norm than the exception in countless ancient pagan cultures.

The Mayans believed any child offered as a sacrifice would exist in some resurrected form. Mass child sacrifice occurred in northern Peru with a tribe called Moche. One of the Andean gods was Ekeko; and to his honor, children were offered. Plutarch wrote about child sacrifice in Carthage, describing the gruesome act of slitting throats before throwing the children into the fire. The Quran (6:137–40) condemns pre-Muslim pagan Arabs who likewise sacrificed their children in the name of Allah.

Traces of child cannibalism can also be found in certain periods of human history, including premodern Europe, southern Africa, and Uganda. These dark aspects of the world's religious history reveal the extent to which unbelieving people will go in forsaking the true worship of God—plus the disastrous consequences such gross rebellion against God can bring upon subsequent generations of children.

A sinister kind of child sacrifice is also a common practice—on a massive scale—in our own culture. Abortion has virtually become the principle sacrament of today's secular religion. If you doubt that, notice the religious fervor with which feminists and politicians defend—even *celebrate*—abortion as if it were a positive good. Once universally deemed an iniquity that even its advocates said should be made safe and legal but kept rare, abortion is now widely promoted as an everyday necessity and an enormous benefit to society. "Healthcare," they call it. A well-known Hollywood actress made headlines in 2016 when she said she regretted *not* having an abortion. "I still haven't had an abortion," she said, "but I wish I had." For her, abortion would have been a ritual, sacrificial, public expression of her faith in the secular, feminist belief system that serves as a surrogate religion in her way of thinking. It is the exact equivalent of ancient pagan child sacrifices.

Mothers' wombs—designed for the nurture and protection of unborn babies—are now literally the most dangerous place of all for millions of unborn children. Millions of children conceived in America have been aborted before birth. A preborn baby today has a massive probability of being murdered in the womb rather than surviving until birth.

Indeed, the womb is where the first and most deadly assault in the war on children has its inception. Satan's assault starts there and never lets up. The normalization of abortion—the idea that children are disposable, inconvenient, and some kind of existential threat to health and happiness—has so devalued the perception of a child's worth that it is no wonder so many children worldwide are neglected, abused, and exposed to evil by the very people who should be protecting them. Every conceivable medium seems to collude to undermine the innocence and well-being of children: broken homes, sinful parents, every form of media, the educational system—even the medical world. Children are subjected to damaging influences wherever they turn.

The war on children is also a sinister, supernatural war against God because (as we have seen) children belong to Him. That truth is highlighted in Mark 10:13–16:

> They were bringing children to Him so that He might touch them; but the disciples rebuked them. But when Jesus saw this, He was indignant and said to them, "Permit the children to come to Me; do not hinder them; for the kingdom of God belongs to such as these. Truly I say to you, whoever does not receive the kingdom of God like a child will not enter it at all." And He took them in His arms and began blessing them, laying His hands on them.

The culture in Jesus' time appears to have shown comparatively little interest in children. Its theology of meritorious good works seemed to exclude children, since they couldn't perform righteous deeds. At a certain point, the boys were formally inducted as sons of the law when they turned thirteen at their *bar mitzvah*. But overall, the children's spiritual welfare was largely neglected.[10]

However, according to the Talmud, it was customary once a year for parents to bring their children to the Temple or to a synagogue for a special blessing just before the Day of Atonement. Parents valued formal blessings from fathers, prophets, and rabbis. So the Jewish elders would lay hands on the child's head, one by one, offering blessings and praying for the child's future growth, including fame in the law, faithfulness in marriage, and abundance in good works.

Something like that had prompted this incident in Mark 10 (recorded also in parallel accounts found in Matthew 19 and Luke 18). Parents—evidently there were many—were bringing their children to Jesus, hoping for Jesus to touch them with heavenly blessing. They had seen Him heal with a touch, so they knew He had divine power.

When the disciples rebuked them (thinking, perhaps, that this parade of parents with children constituted an inconvenience or an interruption of the Lord's ministry), Jesus Himself became indignant. When He said, "Permit the children to come to Me... the kingdom of God belongs to such as these," it was stunning. It flatly contradicted the view that children were insignificant.

Jesus lovingly embraced the children, blessing them and laying His hands upon them, affirming their place in His kingdom. (Remember that in Ezekiel, God refers to them as "My children.") Jesus even said that *all* sinners must receive the kingdom of God with childlike faith—thus elevating the sacred value of a little child's simple, innocent, unquestioning trust.

Psalm 127:3 makes this unqualified declaration: "Behold, children are a gift of the LORD." That is the same text that goes on to say children are a valuable treasure and a reward, comparable to arrows in the hands of a warrior. The psalmist praises the man whose quiver is full of children, emphasizing the strength and honor children bring to a family.

In Psalm 139, David acknowledges God's omniscience, recognizing that the Lord knows every aspect of our being—from the womb:

> O LORD, You have searched me and known me. You know when I sit down and when I rise up; You understand my thought from afar. You scrutinize my path and my lying down, and are intimately acquainted with all my ways....
>
> You formed my inward parts; You wove me in my mother's womb. I will give thanks to You, for I am fearfully and wonderfully made; wonderful are Your works, and my soul knows it very well. My frame was not hidden from You, when I was made in secret, and skillfully wrought in the depths of

the earth; Your eyes have seen my unformed substance; and
in Your book were all written the days that were ordained for
me, when as yet there was not one of them.

How precious also are Your thoughts to me, O God!
(vv. 1–3; 13–17)

David is confessing that God created and therefore knew every
detail of his gifts and personality when David was just a zygote.
As a created being, he belongs to God.

In Psalm 22:9, David says to God, "You are He who brought
me forth from the womb." So Scripture is quite clear on this:
God's care for little ones begins at conception. Throughout the
Bible, from Genesis onward, the birth of a child is consistently
viewed as an act of God. This divine involvement is evident
in various instances, such as Ishmael's birth to an unbeliever
(Genesis 16:2–4; 17:20) and the conception of Ruth's son by divine
enablement (Ruth 4:13). Hannah's conception of Samuel is also
attributed to the Lord (1 Samuel 1:19–20).

Therefore, when Jesus demonstrated His care and concern
for children by taking a child in His arms, He was simply
demonstrating the character of God. (He is, after all, God in
human flesh.) But this was not merely for show. Jesus' response
on this occasion was a sincere reflection of His own deep love,
care, and appreciation for children.

It was also a public challenge to the narrow perspective of
that culture. Mark weaves a subtle thread of this subject into his
gospel. In Mark 9:36, he tells us that Jesus took a child in His
arms. A chapter later, in Mark 10:16, it is now multiple children,
as it says, "He took them in His arms and began blessing them,
laying His hands on them." Obviously, then, these were very

young children. While Matthew and Mark use the term *paidion,* which can refer to a child of any age, Luke 18:15 specifically says, "They were bringing even their babies [*brephos*] to Him so that He would touch them." They were no doubt seeking a supernatural blessing from this remarkable worker of signs and wonders.

To their dismay, however, "the disciples rebuked them" (Mark 10:13). The Greek verb for "rebuked" is *epitimaō,* and it conveys the idea of a stern reprimand. (The word is often associated with punishment.) In other words, the disciples vehemently opposed the parents' actions.

From verse 14, it is evident that Jesus reacted strongly: "He was indignant." It probably does not overstate the case to say He was angered by the disciples' attempt to deter those parents. This was not a trivial matter. The disciples' disregard for children was at odds with God's own tender care for little ones. Jesus' answer in verse 14 was probably spoken with the tone of a sharp rebuke, "Permit the children to come to Me; do not hinder them; for the kingdom of God belongs to such as these."

That statement is truly remarkable. Jesus did not merely say, "The kingdom of God belongs to these," implying that these particular children were elect—chosen by God for salvation. Instead, He asserts, "The kingdom of God belongs to *such as these*"—referring to a whole category of humanity: children in general.

Notably, there is no mention of the parents' faith, nor is there any discussion of a covenant, baptism, circumcision, or any specific ritual. If there were ever an appropriate moment to address infant baptism, it would have been here. Yet Jesus remains completely silent on the matter.

"The kingdom of God *belongs* to such as these." That suggests that little children, too young to have an adult sense of moral awareness, too young to believe the gospel meaningfully or reject it deliberately—such children *belong to God,* and that's why His kingdom belongs to them. God cares in a special, unique, gracious sense for children who are too young to make their own moral choices.

He says so expressly in the final chapter of Jonah. The prophet is pouting and indignant because he wanted to see Nineveh overthrown by God's judgment, but the people had repented. The Lord chastens the wayward prophet for his lack of compassion, and in the final verse of the book of Jonah, God asks the petulant prophet, "Should I not have compassion on Nineveh, the great city in which there are more than 120,000 persons who do not know the difference between their right and left hand?" Those 120,000 persons are children too young to know right from left. God has extraordinary compassion on such little ones. According to Jesus, the kingdom of heaven belongs to them. One of the clear implications of that text is that infants and small children who die are graciously gathered by God into the kingdom. (I've elaborated on this truth elsewhere, in a book titled *Safe in the Arms of God* [Nashville: Nelson, 2003].)

Aren't children born sinners? Doesn't Scripture teach that Adam's sin corrupted all his offspring?

Yes. David makes this confession in Psalm 51:5: "Behold, I was brought forth in iniquity, and in sin my mother conceived me." He didn't mean the act by which he was conceived was sinful; he was confessing that the guilt of humanity's fallenness and a proclivity to sin in his own heart were there from the beginning. In Psalm 58:3 he writes, "The wicked are estranged from the womb." That is speaking not only about some class of extraordinarily wicked people. It applies to all of us: "As it is written, 'There is none righteous, not even one'.... For all have sinned and fall short of the glory of God" (Romans 3:10, 23).

Our inherent sinfulness is not something acquired when we sin willfully. Children are not born morally neutral, as if they *become* sinners when they make their own sinful choices for the first time. All of humanity is fallen. Every human heart in its fallen and unredeemed state is inclined toward sin. Left to our own choices, all of us will sin. Again, "all *have* sinned and fall short of the glory of God."

That is why parents are given the task of bringing their children up "in the discipline and instruction of the Lord" (Ephesians 6:4). It's a task we cannot take lightly, much less ignore. And with so many forces in our culture waging war against children, faithful parents must be more vigilant and more diligent than ever.

I must also emphasize that the people of this current generation who advocate or tolerate the slaughter of unborn infants will ultimately answer to God. So will all those who perpetrate immoral acts against children—including so many public school officials who seem inordinately eager to expose children to sexual perversions and unholy values. They will discover that "It is a terrifying thing to fall into the hands of the living God" (Hebrews 10:31). "For our God is a consuming fire" (12:29).

Jesus made a formal pronouncement of woe against those who deliberately cause spiritual injury to His children. Of the person who perpetrates such an offense, He said, "It would be better for him if a millstone were hung around his neck and he were thrown into the sea, than that he would cause one of these little ones to stumble" (Luke 17:2). He is of course speaking of all who trust Him. Even adult believers are His children—childlike, because the faith by which they embrace Christ savingly is a simple, pure, ingenuous trust. But Jesus' warning about "caus[ing] little ones to stumble" certainly applies as well to anyone who would purposely inflict spiritual damage or moral corruption—or any kind of harm—on a literal child.

Christian parents, on the other hand, have no need to fear the fire of God's wrath (Romans 8:1), but we *will* be held accountable by Him for the little ones He entrusts to our care. Our children are not ours alone, or even ultimately. They belong to God, and our lifelong commitment is to make sure that we teach and influence them regarding God's will and the gospel of salvation.

# CHAPTER THREE

# HAMPERED BY THE CURSE OF SIN

The war on children is not a new phenomenon, but it has lately escalated to catastrophic levels. Over the past half-century or longer, educational institutions (with eager support from the government, media, and big business) have played a major part in a subtle but coordinated campaign to undermine the family unit and commandeer the minds and hearts of children. Now, however, the pretense of subtlety is gone. Public schools are openly fighting to minimize parental influence in the educational process. Gender-bending ideological indoctrination is being aggressively force-fed to the very youngest schoolchildren. School libraries routinely include books targeting children, featuring imagery and detailed descriptions of sexual perversions that are so inappropriate they can't be read in open sessions of Congress or shown on broadcast television without being blurred and bleeped by network censors. But school officials have angrily contended that they have a legal right—even a duty as educators—to make sure such literature remains easily available to elementary-level students. In many school districts, indoctrinating children to accept all kinds of sexual perversions has become a priority over teaching math, history, reading, and other subjects that used to be considered core curriculum.

Throughout history, Satan and the forces of darkness have always sought to destroy children, drawing them into the shadows of evil and immorality and away from the light of truth and decency. Children, being the most vulnerable among us, are prime targets for the enemy of our souls. They bear the crippling disadvantage of human fallenness, and they are therefore naturally enticed by evil. Any experienced parent understands that children do not gravitate naturally toward what is good. Their curiosity and energies must be guided toward honor, integrity, and morality.

Of course, the very notion of righteousness is meaningless apart from God, and Scripture is the ultimate authority that defines what righteousness is. So once a culture abandons biblical values, it becomes impossible to shield children from evil influences.

Our culture is on the cusp of that dilemma right now. It is crucial for those who believe God's Word and love righteousness to take the lead in nurturing and protecting our children. This is a task that is vital to our calling as the people of God.

In the biblical creation account, we read, "God created man in His own image, in the image of God He created him; male and female He created them. God blessed them; and God said to them, 'Be fruitful and multiply'" (Genesis 1:27–28). So the Lord intended for men and women to marry, procreate, and bring up righteous children.

However, Adam disobeyed the one restriction God gave him. He fell, and with him the entire human race was plunged into sin. Adam's sin also brought a curse on all of creation. In pronouncing that curse, God told the woman, "I will greatly multiply your pain in childbirth, in pain you will bring forth children" (Genesis 3:16). So God's creation mandate was not revoked. Men and women were still supposed to marry and bear children, but childbirth would be accompanied by suffering.

"Now the man called his wife's name Eve, because she was the mother of all the living" (v. 20). Eve was of course the first to bear children. The creation mandate to "be fruitful and multiply, and fill the earth" remained, but the process would be grievously affected by sin. Just one chapter later, in Genesis 4, jealousy between the first two siblings in the original family led one brother to murder the other. Beginning with the very first generation after Adam, humanity was severely marred by the very worst kinds of dysfunction and broken relationships.

Complications of the Fall, the curse, and the consequences of sin quickly took hold within the hearts of all Adam's offspring—and those difficulties endure even today.

The book of Genesis goes on to recount the series of broken families, unfaithful marriages, and victimized children that characterized human life. The catastrophic record of human failure and dysfunctional family relationships runs from Cain, the murderer (Genesis 4:1–16); to Lamech, the first polygamist who boasted about his lifestyle through poetry (vv. 19–24); to the days of Noah, when corruption ran rampant and led to God's decision to drown the entire human race with a global flood, sparing only eight individuals (6:1–7). It is astounding how soon after the Fall God had to bring about the destruction of humanity because of pervasive corruption. He left only a remnant of one family, from which life could begin anew.

God's judgment on humanity continued after the Flood at the Tower of Babel, where God (by supernaturally multiplying languages) confounded the efforts of the earliest globalists to establish a false one-world religion (11:1–9). The judgment at Babel ended the original collaboration against God and scattered people in confusion.

Following that, Genesis describes the troubled marriage between Abraham and Sarah. Even with the birth of Isaac by a divine miracle, Abraham's household was far from being an ideal family. The relationship between Abraham and Sarah was marred by adultery and the birth of Ishmael, an illegitimate son. Moreover, the very next generation was rendered dysfunctional by the conflict between Jacob and Esau. And in the generation after that, Jacob's sons sold their brother Joseph into slavery out of jealousy.

Genesis concludes with Joseph in a coffin in Egypt. So according to Scripture, from the very start, the human race has been plagued with pervasive war within families and against children. In short, there is no record of a truly healthy, godly, model family in the entire book of Genesis. And this is the story of the biblical patriarchs, from whom the people of God would emerge. Abraham is called the father of true faith, but his family had serious problems, and his children committed grievous sins. This illustrates what a difficult thing it is for even the most faithful parents to raise their children in the nurture and admonition of the Lord. Our own sin can hinder us.

In other words, family life itself is already challenging because even the best parents are themselves sinners. On top of that colossal disadvantage has been piled all the mischief perpetrated by the kingdom of darkness, led by Satan himself. The onslaught of evil against children is further amplified by a worldly culture that forcefully promotes wickedness and aims its fiercest hostility directly against the biblical ideal of marriage and the family.

All of that is precisely how Western culture today, having shed the vestiges of biblical morality, has joined the devil's assault against children—with a determination that most would have thought impossible a decade or two ago. All the forces of sin, both internal and external, relentlessly strive to destroy the family. It should be clear by now that children are the chief victims of the resulting devastation.

As we noted in the previous chapter, pagan cultures in ancient times offered their children as human sacrifices to their gods— and shockingly, even the descendants of Abraham forsook God and followed the horrific idolatrous practices of their neighbors, frequently adopting the pagan practice of ritual child sacrifices. And as we saw, the Lord regards that as one of the most egregious of all sins because every child is His creation, and each child therefore belongs to Him in a unique sense.

God Himself freely gives children an extra measure of divine grace, and because they are born into a fallen race, their need for His grace is of course profound. But as stewards of the children God has entrusted to our care, we also have a high and holy duty to give them nurture, protection, and instruction. They urgently need instruction in righteousness, because as they grow into adulthood, they will become responsible for their own moral choices.

The distinction between young children and responsible adults is clearly seen in 2 Samuel 12, when David's illegitimate baby son, conceived through an adulterous relationship with Bathsheba, was struck with a dire sickness. After a week the child died, and Scripture says David, who had fasted in sorrow and laid all night on the ground for those seven days—

arose from the ground, washed, anointed himself, and changed his clothes; and he came into the house of the LORD and worshiped. Then he came to his own house, and when he requested, they set food before him and he ate.

Then his servants said to him, "What is this thing that you have done? While the child was alive, you fasted and wept; but when the child died, you arose and ate food." He said, "While the child was still alive, I fasted and wept; for I said, 'Who knows, the LORD may be gracious to me, that the child may live.' But now he has died; why should I fast? Can I bring him back again? I will go to him, but he will not return to me." (vv. 20–23)

David knew that his little one was safe in the arms of the God to whom he belonged. David also understood that he would one day be reunited with the child in heaven.

In stark contrast, just a few chapters later, in 2 Samuel 18, David's rebellious adult son Absalom was brutally killed. The thirty third verse of that chapter describes David's profound sorrow and anguish, knowing that although he would again see the infant son who had died, he would never see wicked Absalom.

Those who sacrificed children in Old Testament times did so for selfish and materialistic reasons. They thought sacrificing their children would guarantee their own security and prosperity. They believed the gods they worshiped with such sacrificial devotion would give them good fortune, and they were willing to burn their own children to death in order to escape the anger of the idol-god and gain whatever benefits they believed their imaginary deity would give them.

People today *still* prioritize their own desires at the expense of their children. The number-one excuse women give for aborting babies is that they regard the duties of motherhood as an inconvenience and interruption to their own life plans.

This is a form of idolatry not significantly different from the paganism of those who slaughtered children in ancient times. Although the objects they worship have changed, the principles are still the same, and the result is also the same. The prevalent idol is *self*. Witness the erosion of religious beliefs in our culture because religions are seen as restrictive. Each person wants to become his or her own deity.

Consequently, children are sacrificed on the altar of self. Unborn children are offered to abortionists as a sacrifice to satisfy the parents' cravings for freedom, lust, pleasure, and selfishness. Born children are surrendered to secular education and the gods of knowledge and foolishness, allowing them to appear wise while behaving in an ungodly manner, after the example set by wicked teachers. Parents sacrifice their children to the priests of immoral entertainment, embracing the gods of perversion who lead vulnerable youths into darkness and the destruction of homosexuality, transgenderism, and pornography. Children are handed over to manipulative liars who control and exploit them through the media, acting as agents and high priests of moral corruption. Parents offer their children to feminists, beta males, woke propagandists and politicians, liars, racists, and deceivers—all as a virtue-signaling sacrifice to a worldly notion of "justice," often simply to gain acceptance from society's trendsetters. This is not how Christians are supposed to order their lives. At the end of the day, this is precisely why "the wisdom of this world is foolishness before God" (1 Corinthians 3:19).

The religious idolatry of our time particularly harms children, but it also ruins marriages, destroys fathers, and overwhelms mothers. These idols are pervasive, and their evil influence is like a lethal chemical weapon spreading through the atmosphere.

How can we best protect our children? The challenge godly parents face may seem insurmountable. Many powerful politicians are clearly on the side of Satan. They are bent on making laws to protect the very vices that destroy children and families. They criminalize truth as hate speech. In many companies, a person's employment will be terminated if he defends marriage as a union between a man and a woman, if he insists there are only two genders, or if he declines to use someone's "preferred pronouns." Girls are summarily cut from sports teams if they complain about having to compete against males who pretend to be women. The culture relentlessly perpetuates lies while censoring and silencing the truth. Conspiracy theories used to be fairly easy to debunk, but we have learned in recent years that whatever government and media are trying their hardest to conceal, cancel, or mock is very often the truth.

Although many of the instruments and influences that have been weaponized in the war against children have been perpetrated by lawmakers and established by political stratagems, no political remedy can offer a true and ultimate solution, or even reverse all these societal trends. How then can we safeguard our children? Let's begin at the very foundation.

First, marriage is life's ultimate blessing. The New Testament calls it "the grace of life" (1 Peter 3:7). After Adam's creation, the Lord said, "It is not good for the man to be alone; I will make him a helper suitable for him" (Genesis 2:18).

> So the LORD God caused a deep sleep to fall upon the man, and he slept; then He took one of his ribs and closed up the

flesh at that place. The LORD God fashioned into a woman the rib which He had taken from the man, and brought her to the man. The man said, "This is now bone of my bones, and flesh of my flesh; she shall be called Woman, because she was taken out of Man." For this reason a man shall leave his father and his mother, and be joined to his wife; and they shall become one flesh. And the man and his wife were both naked and were not ashamed. (vv. 21–25)

Ephesians 5 tells us the relationship between a husband and wife symbolizes Christ's care for and connection to His church. Marriage, without a doubt, is life's primary blessing because of its intensity, longevity, and productivity. For those who deliberately delay marriage, hoping for some perfect mate—as well as for those who put off marrying because they want to pursue some selfish agenda that benefits no one but themselves: *You are missing out on the grace of life.* Marriage is God's ultimate earthly blessing.

Children are a large element of that blessing. Contrary to what many people today assume, a pet is no adequate surrogate for a child. Friends cannot fully satisfy the most profound longings God has designed into the human heart. The extraordinary blessedness of children is highlighted repeatedly in the Bible. It is a major theme, for example, in the story of Leah and Rachel in Genesis 29:31–35:

Now the LORD saw that Leah was unloved, and He opened her womb, but Rachel was barren. Leah conceived and bore a son and named him Reuben, for she said, "Because the LORD has seen my affliction; surely now my husband will love me." Then she conceived again and bore a son and said, "Because the LORD has heard that I am unloved, He has therefore given me this son also." So she named him Simeon. She conceived again and bore a son and said, "Now this time my husband will become attached to me, because I have borne him three sons." Therefore he was named Levi. And she conceived again and bore a son and said, "This time I will praise the LORD." Therefore she named him Judah.

Leah saw her children as divinely given blessings—and indeed, they were.

In Deuteronomy 7:12–13 God gives this command, with a corresponding promise, to Israel: "Then it shall come about, because you listen to these judgments and keep and do them, that the LORD your God will keep with you His covenant and His lovingkindness which He swore to your forefathers. He will love you and bless you and multiply you; He will also bless the fruit of your womb." It is truly a heavenly blessing to have children. Scripture repeatedly makes reference to children as blessings from God. In Psalm 113:9, for example, the psalmist writes, "He makes the barren woman abide in the house as a joyful mother of children. Praise the LORD!"

Children are not a disruption, but rather an incomparable love gift from God.

Psalm 115:14–15 invokes this blessing: "May the LORD give you increase, you and your children. May you be blessed of the LORD, Maker of heaven and earth." And as we noted early in this book, Psalm 127:3–5 states the fact emphatically: "Behold, children are a gift of the LORD, the fruit of the womb is a reward. Like arrows in the hand of a warrior, so are the children of one's youth. How blessed is the man whose quiver is full of them; they will not be ashamed when they speak with their enemies in the gate." Children are indeed a precious reward bestowed by the Lord.

The very next psalm, Psalm 128, highlights the blessings of fearing the Lord and walking in His ways. It declares the happiness and well being that come from enjoying the love of family in a context where faith in the Lord is a family's anchor. Here is the entire psalm:

> How blessed is everyone who fears the LORD, who walks in His ways. When you shall eat of the fruit of your hands, you will be happy and it will be well with you. Your wife shall be like a fruitful vine within your house, your children like olive plants around your table. Behold, for thus shall the man be blessed who fears the LORD.
>
> The LORD bless you from Zion, and may you see the prosperity of Jerusalem all the days of your life. Indeed, may you see your children's children. Peace be upon Israel!

Notice: The man's wife is analogous to a fruitful vine. His children are like lush and fruitful olive plants. His grandchildren will be a crown and honor to him in his advanced years. Contrary to the jaded perspective that views children as hindrances to adult plans, God regards them as His richest benefits in life.

Notice also that fear of the Lord is the condition that makes the man's happiness possible. Marriage and family are the primary blessing in life—but that is true *only for those who trust in the Lord.*

Those who genuinely fear and obey God will therefore invest love and wisdom in their spouse and children. When children are not properly parented, they are always trouble, and nobody is blessed. Parenting is not just giving birth to children, but carefully and diligently leading them to grow up as responsible, God-loving adults.

The book of Proverbs is filled with parental wisdom. Proverbs 10:1 states, "A wise son makes a father glad, but a foolish son is a grief to his mother." Proverbs 29:17 advises parents, "Correct your son, and he will give you comfort; he will also delight your soul." Parenting requires instruction with appropriate consequences.

Proverbs 13:24 emphasizes the crucial role of corporal discipline: "He who withholds his rod hates his son, but he who loves him disciplines him diligently." If you have a child, you've got a little reprobate in your house. No doubt, he or she is a beautiful, adorable little reprobate. That child will not grow up to be a blessing to anyone unless you discipline your son or daughter according to God's design. And Scripture says the proper instrument is a rod.

What that means is that God intends you to inflict pain—not injury, and certainly not wanton abuse, but an appropriate level of pain—as a consequence of misconduct. To be effective, corrective discipline should be immediate and firm, but always administered with love and compassion, not out of cruelty or raw anger. The point of discipline is to benefit our children (Hebrews 12:10), not to exasperate them (Colossians 3:21).

But (contrary to the rules of political correctness currently in force) you cannot properly train children or even show them genuine love without disciplining them. God's own discipline of His people is the model for this. "'Those whom the Lord loves He disciplines, and He scourges every son whom He receives.' It is for discipline that you endure; God deals with you as with sons; for what son is there whom his father does not discipline?" (Hebrews 12:6–7). Proverbs 19:18 therefore urges parents to discipline their children while there is still hope for their best. The point is that neglecting loving parental discipline can lead to the worst.

As a child and as a young person, your son or daughter is defenseless, immature, lacking judgment, discretion, and common sense, *much less* seasoned wisdom. Uncorrected, they are on the fast track to death. Proverbs 22:15 says, "Foolishness is bound up in the heart of a child; the rod of discipline will remove it far from him." Proverbs 23:13–14 likewise reassures parents: "Do not hold back discipline from the child, although you strike him with the rod, he will not die. You shall strike him with the rod and rescue his soul from Sheol." Again, the alternative to discipline is death, because an unruly child is on the short path to dying.

That's why in Exodus 20:12, a promise is appended to the fifth commandment: "Honor your father and your mother, that your days may be prolonged in the land which the LORD your God gives you." The Old Testament's wisdom literature is full of admonitions—especially in the Psalms and Proverbs—teaching us that fearing the Lord, cherishing marriage, embracing children as blessings, and faithfully carrying out the responsibilities of parenting are all part of God's design for a fulfilling and blessed life.

It is important to recognize that God intended parents to be the dominant force and the pervasive influence in shaping a child's worldview and behavior. Parents need to minimize (and often counteract) all other competing forces and influences—from the world, friends, school, and media. In today's culture especially, parents must actively and lovingly strive to make sure their own positive biblical example and instruction remains the principal influence in shaping their children's beliefs and values.

Indeed, this is a sacred duty all parents have. In Deuteronomy 6, parents are commanded to teach their children—*diligently*—to love the Lord with their whole being. This is our calling as parents. Effective parenting is not only a blessing that returns joy to parents' hearts, but it also benefits everyone who interacts with your children. Most importantly, it blesses children by setting them on a path of life rather than a path of destruction.

The New Testament, particularly Ephesians 6, adds depth to this understanding. The opening verse addresses children directly: "Children, obey your parents in the Lord, for this is right." That call for obedience stems from acknowledging the authority parents have in guiding children away from foolishness and toward wisdom. Teach your children to obey because it is right—and rewarding.

Verses 2–3: "Honor your father and mother (which is the first commandment with a promise), so that it may be well with you, and that you may live long on the earth." The apostle Paul is quoting the fifth commandment from Exodus 20:12—and it is indeed the first of the Ten Commandments with a promise attached to it. By honoring parents, children can experience a well lived life and longevity. That is a truism, not an ironclad guarantee. Obviously, not every child of good parents will live to old age, but as a general reality, well-disciplined children who follow the path of wisdom, honor their parents, and obey them can enjoy a fulfilling life and avoid destructive paths.

And finally (Ephesians 6:4): "Fathers, do not provoke your children to anger, but bring them up in the discipline and instruction of the Lord." Although the text uses the word "fathers," the admonition is to all parents—mothers as well. The New Testament succinctly captures the essence of parenting in this one statement.

So the initial three verses of Ephesians 6 focus on the need for a child's submission to parents—obeying and honoring them. A parent's duty is even implied in those instructions for children. As a parent, you want to teach your children to obey and honor you.

And to earn their true respect, you yourself must demonstrate good character.

Ensure that your parental expectations are reasonable and sensible, enforcing both your directions and your restrictions with consequences that your children will genuinely want to avoid. It is crucial to provide a child with guidance, discipline, and instruction rooted in the Lord's ways. By doing so, you help your child embrace the promise of a blessed life.

I am once again drawn to the wisdom of Proverbs, particularly chapter 4, where a father imparts instruction to his sons:

> Hear, O sons, the instruction of a father, and give attention that you may gain understanding, for I give you sound teaching; do not abandon my instruction. When I was a son to my father, tender and the only son in the sight of my mother, then he taught me and said to me, "Let your heart hold fast my words; keep my commandments and live." (vv. 1–4)

That is how a father must instruct his children: *Acquire wisdom! Acquire understanding! Get that in place of your natural foolishness. Do not forget or turn away from the words of my mouth.* That is the proper goal of every parent. It assumes, of course, the parent's duty to be biblically-minded and faithful. The man who gropes his way through life relying on his own instincts and prejudices without a sound understanding of Scripture is not going to be a good father.

Solomon goes on: "Hear, my son, and accept my sayings and the years of your life will be many" (v. 10). There is that same promise. Again, it is not an absolute surety. It is an axiom that describes the way things normally work. The child who learns wisdom is on the path of a fulfilling life rather than on the fast track to disappointment and regret. Solomon explains,

I have directed you in the way of wisdom; I have led you in upright paths. When you walk, your steps will not be impeded; and if you run, you will not stumble. Take hold of instruction; do not let go. Guard her, for she is your life. Do not enter the path of the wicked and do not proceed in the way of evil men. Avoid it, do not pass by it; turn away from it and pass on. For they cannot sleep unless they do evil; and they are robbed of sleep unless they make someone stumble. For they eat the bread of wickedness and drink the wine of violence. But the path of the righteous is like the light of dawn, that shines brighter and brighter until the full day. (vv. 11–18)

The sage recognizes that children have the potential to create the greatest heartbreak and the greatest joy. You cannot guarantee the eternal salvation of your child—that's not yours to do; it is the work of God. But as a parent, you can—you *must*—be the primary instrument in your children's spiritual growth and instruction. Proverbs 22:6 famously says, "Train up a child in the way he should go, even when he is old he will not depart from it." That is yet another truism—a general truth—not a guarantee. But it is normally the case that children grow up to become a reflection of what their parents taught them.

You cannot do anything to guarantee that your children will trust Christ for salvation. Parents are not sovereign. But it is your responsibility to be an example of godly faith, to teach them the gospel, and to exemplify love for all things pure and holy. God does His saving work through human instruments, and parents are the primary ones He has appointed in the training of children. Train your child to honor you and obey God.

Life itself is deadly dangerous to children, and if they reach the age where they are subject to the judgment of God, if they haven't been raised in the instruction and discipline of the Lord, then life becomes even more dangerous.

We dealt with the wicked practice of child sacrifice during Old Testament times in the previous chapter. Male and female children were tortured and then consumed in the fires of the sacrificial Tophet. Artifacts of these sacrificial fires have been found in Sicily, Malta, and Sardinia—Mediterranean islands near Italy. It's interesting to read some of the ancient Greek literature at that time and find no evidence that the Greeks or the Romans were ever critical of such cruelty to children. That reflects the fact that in Paul's day the dominant culture was fundamentally indifferent about what happened to children.

There was, in fact, a Roman legal principle called *patria potestas*, Latin for "the father's power." In ancient Rome, fathers held complete authority over their children. They had the power to sell them into slavery, subject them to hard labor, and even inflict cruel and injurious punishments. Shockingly, there were no laws protecting children from abuse, and fathers even had the right to kill their own offspring regardless of age. Newborns would be brought to their fathers, and the father would either acknowledge or reject the child. Thus fathers were believed to have every right to determine whether their children would live or die. Unwanted children would be abandoned in the Roman Forum and often collected at night by people who would turn them into slaves or supply brothels with them. Seneca, a renowned ancient Roman writer (4 BC–AD 65), described how casually and dispassionately Roman men during the time of Christ would dispose of their unwanted children:

> No one, surely, hates his limb as he amputates it. His action is not one of anger, just a painful cure. We put down mad dogs;

we kill the wild, untamed ox; we use the knife on sick sheep to stop their infecting the flock; we destroy abnormal offspring at birth; *children, too, if they are born weak or deformed, we drown.* Yet this is not the work of anger, but of reason—to separate the sound from the worthless.[11]

In contrast, Scripture calls parents to a far different standard, as we noted in Ephesians 6:4: "Do not provoke your children to anger, but bring them up in the discipline and instruction of the Lord."

One father expressed his approach to that duty this way:

If I could start my parenting journey anew, here's what I would do: I would display more love toward my wife in front of our children. I would embrace laughter, even in our mistakes. I would listen attentively, even to the youngest child. I would be honest about my own imperfections, never pretending to be flawless. I would pray differently for my family, focusing on my own growth instead of solely focusing on them. I would engage in more activities together with my children. I would offer more encouragement and provide instruction from the Word of God. I would pay greater attention to small acts and words.

Lastly, I would passionately share the gospel at every opportunity, every day that God grants me.

There is undeniable wisdom in those words. Children are adorable, but they are, after all, little sinners. As parents we are stewards of their welfare, and that means we have a duty before God to instruct and direct them in the way of righteousness. This corrupt culture is certainly not going to protect your children. On the contrary, society is actively championing everything that will destroy your children. If you embrace your duty as a parent and apply yourself to the task biblically and prayerfully, God will give you grace and wisdom to succeed.

Someone who watched my fourteen-month-old great-grandson take his first little jaunt across the church campus said to me, "It's too bad he was born in such wicked times."

I said, "No, this is his time; he came to the kingdom for such a time as this."

This wretched culture needs the next generation to be virtuous, godly, and wise. It is the duty of parents and grandparents to make that investment together and enjoy the reward of their loving efforts in the children who are a rich blessing.

# CHAPTER FOUR

# CHILDREN ARE A GIFT FROM THE LORD

Children have always been the most vulnerable members of society, since they lack adequate strength and wisdom to fight back. Their innocent naïveté makes them susceptible to deception and harm, rendering them the easiest targets for anyone with evil intentions. And the world today is full of people harboring evil intentions.

Parents possess the profound ability to shape their children's lives, either positively or negatively. They hold the power and influence to exemplify noble character and righteous virtues—or alternatively, to demonstrate dissolute, wicked, and sinful behavior.

Unfortunately, as we have stressed from the very beginning, children bear the consequences of their parents' wrong attitudes and actions. When a society becomes plagued with evil, it is the children who suffer most, generally falling into the same or even worse patterns of sin as their parents. This destructive cycle can persist across multiple generations, making it incredibly challenging to reverse. Remember that the Bible says repeatedly that the sins of parents carry consequences that are visited on the children to the third and fourth generations (Deuteronomy 5:9–10).

Furthermore, from the moment of birth, children face the inherent struggle with sin. That is precisely what David was acknowledging when he wrote, in Psalm 51:5, "I was brought forth in iniquity, and in sin my mother conceived me." He wasn't complaining that the doctrine of original sin is unfair; he was acknowledging and confessing just how deeply ingrained his sin really was.

All children enter the world as sinners. They, like their parents, lack any native ability to restrain their sinful nature. They will sin; they cannot avoid it. It is their nature. Their inexperience, inherent foolishness, defective judgment, and lack of simple prudence further compound this battle, as described in the book of Proverbs.

We have noted already that in addition to grappling with their own fallenness and limited understanding, children inherit a cultural environment that has been shaped by their parents' generation and three or four generations of older ancestors, all of whom were also sinful by nature. So the collective culture will always (to a greater or lesser degree) be formed and fashioned by wickedness. Children also face the more immediate reality of their own parents' failures. Countless kids grow up with a lack of parental love and discipline. They suffer from the effects of divorce, broken homes, and various forms of sin that assault families and render them dysfunctional.

In other words, the adults whose job it is to raise their own children to honor and love the Lord do not themselves obey Him. Thus, sadly, parents are often the ones who inflict the most harm on their children.

That is why it is essential to be reminded again and again that our children ultimately belong to God, and that parenting is a stewardship—a sacred responsibility.

Sadly, only a very small minority of parents uphold their parental responsibility in a manner that honors God and imparts righteousness to the succeeding generation.

Again we see that the bedrock foundation of successful parenting lies in understanding that marriage, children, and parenting are all God-given, and we as parents are accountable to God for how we fulfill the task.

We return now to Ephesians 6 for a closer look, which is the New Testament's principal summary of family duties. It starts with the duty of children toward their parents: "Children, *obey* your parents in the Lord, for this is right. *Honor* your father and mother" (vv. 1–2). Two imperatives, stated in two key verbs: "obey" and "honor." And as we noted in the previous chapter, this presupposes a duty that belongs to parents—namely, that we are responsible to teach our children to be obedient and respectful.

Verse 4 gives wise guidance for that task. Although the verse is addressed to "fathers" as heads of their households, the expression in this context encompasses both parents, because mother and father are both in positions of authority over the children in a well-ordered family. In Hebrews 11:23, the exact same Greek word is translated "parents." The context of that plural noun makes clear that the writer is referring to the care provided by both of Moses's parents. Thus, while the word technically means "fathers," it clearly encompasses a responsibility that is shared by both fathers and mothers.

The instruction is simple and pointed: "Do not provoke your children to anger, but bring them up in the discipline and instruction of the Lord." Or to paraphrase the sense of it: *Raise your children with discipline and instruction grounded in principles of true righteousness that reflect the character of the Lord and biblical values, and don't unnecessarily frustrate them in the process.* That one command encapsulates the whole responsibility of parents. The goal is to raise children with truth and discipline, enabling them to experience the blessings promised in life.

Teaching obedience and honor toward parents ensures a flourishing life for the child. To raise a generation of godly, blessed children and break the cycle of repeating the fathers' sins, "the discipline and instruction of the Lord" constitute indispensable ingredients.

So let's examine Ephesians 6:4 more closely. Again, though it applies to both parents, the command uses the masculine expression ("fathers") because in the divine design for families, the father is the head. There are of course many cases where because of death or abandonment, the mother is left to care for her children alone. God gives special grace to widows and single parents. But the ideal (indeed, the norm) is clear from Scripture, and it involves two parents. Thus Proverbs says, "Hear, my son, your father's instruction and do not forsake your mother's teaching" (Proverbs 1:8).

Remember, Paul was living and writing in a world where child abuse was common and generally accepted. As we saw in the previous chapter, fathers held supreme power in the family—*patria potestas*—including absolute power in the question of whether a child should live or die. Because fathers throughout the Roman world were commonly assumed to have authority (on a whim, if he felt like it) to goad, torment, or even kill a child, the command includes this negative restraint: "Do not provoke your children to anger."

Colossians 3:21 is the parallel text: "Do not exasperate your children, so that they will not lose heart." The idea is to avoid antagonizing them. The term in the Greek text is strong—"provoke...to anger." It denotes an intense feeling of hostility, animosity, and resentment. Prolonged or repeated provocation from parents fuels that kind of seething anger in the child, and that does far more than merely damage the parent-child relationship; it severely thwarts the child's spiritual development. Often it prods the child into rebellion, and a rebellious heart foments extreme wickedness. Scripture says, "Rebellion is as the sin of divination [witchcraft], and insubordination is as iniquity and idolatry" (1 Samuel 15:23). Provoking rebellion in one's own children is tantamount to purposely steering them onto the broad road that leads to eternal destruction.

How might a father provoke such resentment in the heart of a child? If you're a parent, you are probably familiar already with the buttons you can push that will provoke your child to anger. Some fathers I have known seem to believe that eliciting anger is beneficial because it means the child has received the message. But the Bible explicitly advises fathers not to take such a destructive approach to parenting.

What typically makes children angry? One common danger is *overprotection*. In your desire to protect them, don't confine them. Don't deprive them of simple freedoms. Don't show them a perpetual lack of trust. Don't impose countless rules that make them feel hopelessly restricted. Children never perceive such actions as acts of love—nor is it true love to hover oppressively or remove from your children every choice that they might make for themselves. You do not need to become tyrannical, nor do you need to cosset and confine your children in order to protect them. It is vital for them to have room to grow and become responsible for their own choices. A certain amount of freedom is essential if you expect them to develop responsibility.

Another way parents inadvertently frustrate and provoke their children is through *favoritism*. It is damaging to say things like, "I wish you could be as good as your sister." This type of comparison diminishes the child's perception of your love, leading them to feel inferior and undermining healthy self-confidence. It is never wise to compare your children with each other. Each child is unique and deserves to be given full love without being unfavorably compared to siblings.

Parents often exasperate their children with *unrealistic expectations*. This is a common occurrence in some cultures, and in high-functioning families. Children are pressured always to achieve straight A's and A-pluses. Anything less is met with disappointment or even punishment. Some parents don't care as much about their kids' academic success, but they put the same kind of pressure on their children by demanding a high level of athletic achievement.

Unreasonable expectations place undue constraints on children. Parental demands for excellence might stem initially from a natural, legitimate desire for parents to see their children succeed, but when the parents' own craving for something to boast about eclipses any righteous concern for the total welfare of the child, those high standards we set for our kids can be more hurtful than helpful. It's important to remember that your children may not necessarily attain or surpass your own achievements. Don't anger them by burdening them with the weight of your own ambition and pride.

I remember visiting a girl in the psychiatric ward at UCLA after her suicide attempt. She had asked to meet with a pastor, but the psychiatrist initially hesitated to let me in because she was in a padded cell and doctors considered her a danger to herself. I persisted, however, and I eventually gained access. (I questioned the effectiveness of her treatment, emphasizing that being isolated from human contact in a padded cell wouldn't solve the underlying issue.) They finally allowed me to speak with her, and I managed to break through the facade she had put up for the psychiatrist.

I asked her about what was happening in her heart and encouraged her to open up to me. She revealed that she felt that no matter what she did, it was never enough for her parents. Her fundamental desire to live had been crushed by her own parents, who had relentlessly fueled the feeling that nothing she did would ever be good enough.

It is vital for children to feel they are pleasing their parents. They can usually face coldness, apathy, rejection, even scorn from teachers, friends, or others if they are certain of their parents' affection. But children will never develop any strength or stability if they never receive anything but disapproval and disappointment from their own parents. Unrealistic expectations can make them feel like failures, leading to self injury—or possibly even suicide. This situation is sadly familiar to those who deal with teenagers.

Another similar way to provoke your children unnecessarily is by provoking *discouragement* in their hearts. Don't lash out at them in frustration. Don't dampen their spirits with harsh words or cruel putdowns. Phrases like "You'll never amount to anything!" or "Are you brain-dead?" are all too common in parenting. The same can be said of parents who practice negative reinforcement by withholding thanks, rewards, or approval. Don't hesitate to give your children approval when they deserve it; it is right to show them love and honor whenever you can. Love your children the way God loves us—with grace. God loves us despite our weaknesses, showering us with abundant love as an act of grace.

*Selfishness* is another factor that can exasperate your children. Some parents find it hard to make sacrifices for their children, but that's a recipe for failed parenting. Sacrificing for your children is an essential aspect of love—from the moment they are born until they leave home—and throughout the rest of their lives as well. Authentic love is sacrificial by definition.

When you never sacrifice your plans for your child's desires or needs, they may think you perceive them as an obstacle to your happiness. They might conclude that you are angry or resentful that they're intruding into your life. Show them sacrificial love and generosity through your words and actions; otherwise, they may grow from anger to resentment.

*Impatience* is another common way parents exasperate their children. Allow them to be children, make mistakes, spill things, break things, and share their wild ideas and desires without condemnation or angry words. Don't expect them to think like adults all the time. Instead, affirm their ability to think and express themselves. This fosters hope and a healthy environment for their contentment.

*Neglect* is one of the very worst ways to harm children and exasperate them. Ensure that you spend time with them and show genuine interest in their activities. Avoid using withdrawal or seclusion as a form of punishment. Isolating a child communicates rejection. It's like saying, "I don't want to be with you." It essentially puts them in prison where they may sit and contemplate how little love and affection you have for them.

*Verbal abuse* can also greatly upset children. Remember that they have limited vocabulary, while you possess a powerful range of words. Avoid using your superior storehouse of verbal ammunition to crush them with sarcasm, ridicule, or cutting words. Such behavior frustrates and harms them. That is not how love is expressed, nor is it how the Lord loves us.

How can parents avoid saying or doing such things? The clear answer to that question is just a few verses before the command not to exasperate our children. It's found in Ephesians 5:18: "Be filled with the Spirit." Give the Holy Spirit full control over your life.

Parents face behavior that can be unpredictable, so it's important to react in a Spirit-led manner. While some aspects of child rearing require intentional planning, many moments elicit spontaneous responses that can be hurtful. Choose to react with the Spirit's guidance rather than in the flesh.

The environment children experience in the home shapes their character. Much of what we exemplify and teach to our children is communicated through the unscripted moments of life. So instead of provoking anger, provide loving care for your children.

You have no doubt heard this poetic series of aphorisms by Dorothy Law Nolte:

> If children live with criticism, they learn to condemn.
> If children live with hostility, they learn to fight.
> If children live with fear, they learn to be apprehensive.
> If children live with pity, they learn to feel sorry for themselves.
> If children live with ridicule, they learn to feel shy.
> If children live with jealousy, they learn to feel envy.
> If children live with shame, they learn to feel guilty.
> If children live with encouragement, they learn confidence.
> If children live with tolerance, they learn patience.
> If children live with praise, they learn appreciation.
> If children live with acceptance, they learn to love.
> If children live with approval, they learn to like themselves.
> If children live with recognition, they learn it is good to
>     have a goal.

> If children live with sharing, they learn generosity.
> If children live with honesty, they learn truthfulness.
> If children live with fairness, they learn justice.
> If children live with kindness and consideration,
>     they learn respect.
> If children live with security, they learn to have faith in
>     themselves and in those about them.
> If children live with friendliness, they learn the world is a
>     nice place in which to live.[12]

All of that is true. For Christian parents, however, an even more important truth must be borne in mind: If children live with godly nurture and discipline, they learn biblical values.

That is the positive aspect of the parents' duty, given also in Ephesians 6:4: "Bring them up in the discipline and instruction of the Lord." "Discipline" is translated from a Greek word that refers to child care and training, involving instruction, rewards, and punishments. It is the same word that is likewise translated "discipline" in Hebrews 12:6 and its context: "Those whom the Lord loves He disciplines, and He scourges every son whom He receives."

Again and again, the biblical examples demonstrate that teaching children involves guiding their thoughts, speech, and behavior with both rewards and chastening. However, parents must always ensure that parental love is never treated as a bonus to be given or taken away as a reward or a punishment.

As Hebrews 12 implies, physical punishment is consistent with genuine love, and indeed, corporal punishment is sometimes warranted in parenting. Remember that Proverbs 22:15 says, "Foolishness is bound up in the heart of a child; the rod of discipline will remove it far from him." A chapter later, we read, "Do not hold back discipline from the child, although you strike him with the rod, he will not die. You shall strike him with the rod and rescue his soul from Sheol" (23:13–14). The book of Proverbs contains several similar admonitions to parents. The principle is well summarized by the saying, "Spare the rod and spoil the child." The idea is that the child learns to associate pain with egregiously wrong thinking, speaking, and behaving, so he avoids the acts that result in it.

The Greek term in Ephesians 6:4 translated "instruction," *nouthesia*, denotes verbal guidance accompanied by words of warning. So the expressions "discipline" and "instruction" aren't really dissimilar. They describe not two distinct things, but one style of instruction, emphasized by repetition with a close synonym. But there are two aspects to this type of careful parental instruction. *Negatively*, you train children through rewards and punishments. *Positively*, you educate them with wise instruction.

If there is a slight distinction in the two terms, it is this: "Discipline" encompasses your actions toward them, while "instruction" relates to the words you communicate. The ultimate goal is for them to obey their parents who are teaching them in accordance with biblical principles.

That reality is expressed by the phrase "of the Lord." Children should obey their parents because that aligns with what the Lord requires. It is the righteous thing to do. And in doing so, not only will they please the Lord, but they will also honor their father and mother and move toward a fulfilling life.

As for parents, they have no more-important obligation before God than the spiritual upbringing of their children. Going back to the Old Testament, remember that this is one of the principle commands built into the Shema, that short preamble to Moses's law that is so familiar as a Jewish confession of faith:

Hear, O Israel! The LORD is our God, the LORD is one! You shall love the LORD your God with all your heart and with all your soul and with all your might. These words, which I am commanding you today, shall be on your heart. *You shall teach them diligently to your sons and shall talk of them when you sit in your house and when you walk by the way and when you lie down and when you rise up.* You shall bind them as a sign on your hand and they shall be as frontals on your forehead. You shall write them on the doorposts of your house and on your gates. (Deuteronomy 6:4–9)

That text gives comprehensive instructions for parenting in a very compact form. It calls for a continual process of dialogue and instruction aimed at building the moral precepts of God's law into the heart, mind, conscience, and worldview of a child. Moses reiterates the parents' assignment five chapters later, with the same stress on the unflagging continuity and consistency that parents must maintain in the training of their children: "You shall therefore impress these words of mine on your heart and on your soul…. You shall teach them to your sons, talking of them when you sit in your house and when you walk along the road and when you lie down and when you rise up" (Deuteronomy 11:18–19).

Almost every time Moses admonished Israel about the necessity of keeping God's law, he stressed the importance of teaching the law's moral principles with unfailing diligence to each new generation. In his farewell speech to the people whom he had brought on a forty-year journey through the wilderness, Moses said:

Only give heed to yourself and keep your soul diligently, so that you do not forget the things which your eyes have seen and they do not depart from your heart all the days of your life; but *make them known to your sons and your grandsons.* Remember the day you stood before the LORD your God at Horeb, when the LORD said to me, "Assemble the people to Me, that I may let them hear My words so they may learn to fear Me all the days they live on the earth, *and that they may teach their children.*" (Deuteronomy 4:9–10)

So the well-being of each new generation hinged on how diligently parents instructed their children with biblical truth. Of course, each individual had a duty to understand, meditate on, and carefully obey the moral precepts of God's law in order to guard their own souls. But parents especially had an additional, vitally important, two-pronged duty—namely, to teach their children what God's Word requires, and to hold them to that standard. The constant repetition of this charge was purposeful and appropriate because the cost of failure was national catastrophe. In Moses's words, "You shall keep His statutes and His commandments which I am giving you today, that it may go well with you and with your children after you" (v. 40).

Biblical parenting is not a responsibility that can be handed off to surrogates. No school, no teacher, no church youth group, and no religious tutor can fill the role of spiritual leadership God designed for parents. Many other influences will try to commandeer the parents' function or derail the process of shaping the child's values and beliefs. Parents cannot be passive. They must, above all, be diligent.

Indeed, the adverb *diligently* is one of the key features of the Bible's instructions to parents in Deuteronomy 6:7: "You shall teach [the precepts of God's Word] *diligently* to your sons and shall talk of them when you sit in your house and when you walk by the way and when you lie down and when you rise up."

That command echoes what Moses had already said in Deuteronomy 4:9: "Give heed to yourself and keep your soul *diligently*...[and make God's truth] known to your sons and your grandsons." Those are two different words in the Hebrew text, but both words have militant overtones. "Diligently" in Deuteronomy 6:7 is the English translation of a word that means "to sharpen or whet"—as one would do with the tools of warfare. "Diligently" in Deuteronomy 4:9 translates a Hebrew word that speaks of force or vehemence. Moses is purposely using martial language in order to stress the inescapable reality that parenting is a task analogous to that of military sentry.

Parents must remain on guard full-time. They must be prepared to fight for their children when necessary. And they must be intentional, careful, conscientious, devoted, tireless, and tenacious—"that the generation to come might know, even the children yet to be born...that they should put their confidence in God and not forget the works of God, but keep His commandments" (Psalm 78:6–7).

Raising children in a fallen world is by no means an easy task, especially in a society (like ours) dominated by forces that openly, militantly oppose the truth and moral principles God has revealed in His Word. But the importance of that duty cannot be overstated, and that fact is underscored by the way this charge to parents is repeated over and over in Scripture. Never has it been more urgent for believing parents than it is right now. We must also realize that this is war, and respond accordingly.

What is the starting point for instructing our children about spiritual matters? Obviously, we want them to understand the gospel. But where do we begin? The answer to that question is built into the Shema: "The LORD is our God, the LORD is one!"

Begin by teaching your children the truth that there is only one God. There is no other God but Him. There are not multiple paths to righteousness. There is only one way, and Christ is the living embodiment of that way. He Himself says, "I am the way, and the truth, and the life; no one comes to the Father but through Me" (John 14:6).

Jesus referred to Deuteronomy 6:5 ("You shall love the LORD your God with all your heart and with all your soul and with all your might") as "the great and foremost commandment" (Matthew 22:38). Parents are therefore responsible to teach their children first and foremost to love the Lord their God above everything and everyone else.

Moses goes on in Deuteronomy 6 to say that the degree to which we are faithful to these most fundamental aspects of God's instruction will determine the degree to which we receive His blessing. You as a parent do this so "that it may be well with you" (v. 3). Again in verse 18: "You shall do what is right and good in the sight of the LORD, that it may be well with you."

In other words, the obedience we ask our children to render to us as parents is what the Lord has designed so that they can receive His blessing. It's not for us; it's for the Lord, and it puts our children in a position where they can be blessed. Their own love for the Lord is the essential goal for children, following the example of their parents.

Verse 6 requires a true commitment to obey: "These words, which I am commanding you today, shall be on your heart." God requires obedience from the depths of the heart. True obedience comes only from a heart that loves Him and desires to follow His commands.

Verse 7 stresses the unending responsibility parents have for the instruction of their children. There is quite literally no time off from parenthood. As a parent, you are supposed to teach your children God's truth, and keep talking about that truth, in every aspect of life: "when you sit in your house and when you walk by the way and when you lie down and when you rise up." Literally every moment becomes an opportunity to educate them about the one true God whom they are to love and obey.

Additionally, the text advises us to use reminders everywhere: "Bind them as a sign on your hand and...as frontals on your forehead.... Write them on the doorposts of your house and on your gates" (vv. 8–9). In other words, take care—repeatedly and consistently—to set before yourself and your children visible reminders to love and obey the one true God.

Moses's instructions continue (vv. 10–12):

> Then it shall come about when the LORD your God brings you into the land which He swore to your fathers, Abraham, Isaac and Jacob, to give you, great and splendid cities which you did not build, and houses full of all good things which you did not fill, and hewn cisterns which you did not dig, vineyards and olive trees which you did not plant, and you eat and are satisfied, then watch yourself, that you do not forget the LORD who brought you from the land of Egypt, out of the house of slavery.

Those verses highlight several subtle dangers that lurk in the world. Not only you as a parent, but also your children as the devil's prey, are in constant battle against an evil world system that relentlessly seeks to undermine what you are trying to achieve for your children. Even the blessings God gives can become a temptation if we love the gifts more than the Giver, or if we trust in material things rather than the One who gives us power to obtain wealth (Deuteronomy 8:18). Meanwhile, the world is not our ally; it is a deadly adversary—and it never stops its hateful aggression. "Do not be surprised, brethren, if the world hates you" (1 John 3:13). You must remember that, and you must teach your children to understand it as well.

When do we begin giving biblical instruction to our sons and daughters? *As soon as possible.* The apostle Paul wrote to Timothy, "From childhood you have known the sacred writings which are able to give you the wisdom that leads to salvation through faith which is in Christ Jesus" (2 Timothy 3:15). That is the ideal. It starts in early childhood with faithful parents like Timothy's mother and grandmother (1:5). They instructed him in the Scriptures from childhood, teaching him the wisdom that leads to salvation through faith in Christ Jesus.

You cannot give them too much gospel truth, nor can you start too early. Begin in infancy with the simplest truths—stressing the fact that God is holy and demands perfect holiness. He hates sin and always punishes it. He will judge the world in righteousness. Sin makes true peace with God impossible, and it destroys peace with others as well. We all have sinned, and therefore we fall far short of the glory of God. Left to ourselves, we are headed for eternal death. Forgiveness is not something we can earn. Heaven is not a reward we can merit. Our only hope is to find a Savior.

The good news of the gospel is that God has graciously provided the Savior we need: His Son, the Lord Jesus Christ, who died to pay the price of sins He did not commit, and who rose again to demonstrate that God has accepted His sacrifice.

When your children must be corrected or disciplined for wrongdoing, even *that* is an opportunity for gospel instruction. Don't just rebuke and punish the wrong behavior; teach your child that genuine repentance means turning from sin because sin dishonors God. When a child's behavior requires those teaching moments involving reproof or correction, it is a perfect occasion to instruct them in righteousness. (Those functions—teaching, reproof, correction, and training in righteousness—are, after all, the very ways God's Word ministers to us, according to 2 Timothy 3:16.) Use the opportunity to remind them how vitally important it is for them to reject anything that dishonors God. Urge them to love and trust Jesus Christ as their Savior. If they live their lives faithfully for Christ's honor, they will honor and obey their parents.

Again, the book of Proverbs serves as a manual for parents seeking to instruct their children wisely. Written precisely to provide wisdom for both fathers and children, Proverbs begins with this preamble in verse form:

> The proverbs of Solomon the son of David, king of Israel:
> To know wisdom and instruction,
> To discern the sayings of understanding,
> To receive instruction in wise behavior,
> Righteousness, justice and equity;
> To give prudence to the naive,
> To the youth knowledge and discretion,
> A wise man will hear and increase in learning,
> And a man of understanding will acquire wise counsel,
> To understand a proverb and a figure,
> The words of the wise and their riddles.
> The fear of the LORD is the beginning of knowledge;
> Fools despise wisdom and instruction. (Proverbs 1:1–7)

Clearly, the aim of Proverbs is to impart wisdom to the young, starting with wise parents who desire to pass down godly wisdom to their children.

The Proverbs often speak with the voice of a parent appealing to a son. The first few chapters all start that way. Proverbs 1:8

begins: "Hear, my son, your father's instruction and do not forsake your mother's teaching." Proverbs 2:1 says, "My son... receive my words." In 3:1, it is written, "My son, do not forget my teaching." Proverbs 4:1 adds, "Hear, O sons, the instruction of a father, and give attention that you may gain understanding." The next three chapters all begin with similar appeals. Thumb through Proverbs, and you will notice the son is repeatedly urged to listen carefully to his father's wisdom. Those pleas set the tone for the entire book. Solomon, who wrote it, is speaking as a father to his own children, urging them to follow the path of wisdom.

There's a tone of passionate urgency in those repeated appeals, and it's fitting, because Solomon himself squandered much of his life by not following his own counsel. No doubt he is writing out of his own bitter experience in Proverbs 8:36, where the voice of wisdom personified warns, "He who sins against me injures himself; all those who hate me love death." Rejecting wisdom comes at a very high cost.

The whole book of Proverbs therefore stresses the importance of listening to one's parents' instructions and holding godly wisdom close to the heart. In an echo of Deuteronomy 6, the Proverbs emphasize the significance of attentiveness and compliance to the commandments.

Children are foolish and naïve, desperately in need of wisdom. Remember, Proverbs 22:15 says, "Foolishness is bound up in the heart of a child." Proverbs 12:15 says, "The way of a fool is right in his own eyes." A child in his immaturity may think he's right, but it is the task of a parent to establish wisdom in the place of foolishness in the child's mind and heart.

Salvation alone can bring this wisdom permanently into the child's own heart. According to 1 Corinthians 1:30, "wisdom from God" is embodied in Christ. So when a person is united with Christ by faith, Christ becomes for that person the living source of true and eternal wisdom, for "in [Him] are hidden all the treasures of wisdom and knowledge" (Colossians 2:3). We want our children to have the mind of Christ (1 Corinthians 2:16), and we want them to think accordingly.

Given that the most essential principles of parenting are distilled in the book of Proverbs via pithy but supremely helpful sayings, what would we identify as the key verse—the propositional statement—for the whole book? The obvious choice is Proverbs 1:7: "The fear of the LORD is the beginning of knowledge; fools despise wisdom and instruction." A similar statement is made in Proverbs 9:10: "The fear of the LORD is the beginning of wisdom, and the knowledge of the Holy One is understanding."

Fear of God is not a craven weakness, of course. It is a deep respect and holy awe so profound that it would cause anyone to tremble. There is indeed a measure of righteous terror in the blend of unworthiness and strict accountability that go hand in hand with the true fear of God (2 Corinthians 5:11; Hebrews 10:31). But this is not the fear of gutless contempt or cowardly aversion. It is the kind of fear that provokes profound reverence. It is a holy veneration that chiefly trembles at God's righteous displeasure. That kind of fear is the cornerstone of all true wisdom.

In Luke 12:4–5, Jesus instructs us whom we should fear. He says, "I say to you, My friends, do not be afraid of those who kill the body and after that have no more that they can do. But I will warn you whom to fear: fear the One who, after He has killed, has authority to cast into hell; yes, I tell you, fear Him!" He was saying that God Himself is the one whom we should fear, not men—not even Satan.

And fear God you should, for one thing, because of His omniscience. He knows everything. Jesus goes on to say in verse 6, "Are not five sparrows sold for two cents? Yet not one of them is forgotten before God." If you think you can escape God's all-seeing eyes and therefore you have no reason to fear Him, think again. God even knows what individual sparrows are doing. Christ continues by saying that God knows the precise number of hairs on your head (v. 7). No detail is too small to escape the sovereign knowledge of God. We cannot evade accountability to His judgment.

Children need to understand this truth, precisely because it is the starting point for true wisdom. Parents and Sunday school teachers sometimes try to shield children from the fierce and fearsome attributes of God and the reality of eternal judgment. That is unwise. Notice that Jesus expressly said we are to "fear the One who...has authority to cast into hell." It is important for children to be aware that eternal punishment awaits those who do *not* fear God.

Only when that fear is established can the gospel message come to a sinner as truly good news. In Luke 12, after warning His followers to fear God, Jesus Himself quickly turns to the good news: "I say to you, everyone who confesses Me before men, the Son of Man will confess him also before the angels of God" (v. 8). That is the pattern of wisdom. It starts with fear of God, then turns to the remedy of faith in Christ. It is a pattern every Christian parent should follow as they instruct their children: Fear God, recognize His sovereignty, and confess Jesus as your Savior and Lord because He is the only One who can rescue us from divine wrath.

There is much more that can be said about fearing God and keeping His commandments, but that is the place to start.

Another significant theme in Proverbs is the importance of speaking the truth. True wisdom and truthful speech are inextricably linked. Proverbs 4:24 says, "Put away from you a deceitful mouth and put devious speech far from you."

Lying, of course, is one of the natural expressions of human fallenness. A literal translation of Psalm 58:3 would say, "The wicked have been estranged from the womb. At birth they go astray, speaking falsehood." Every parent knows this truth. Children do not have to be taught how to lie. That comes naturally to them. They must be trained to speak truth.

By the way, righteous speech includes not only truthfulness but every other virtue as well. Children must be taught to speak with kindness, purity, respect, and grace. Proverbs 6:12 says, "A worthless person, a wicked man, is the one who walks with a perverse mouth." Consider these verses: "The mouth of the righteous is a fountain of life, but the mouth of the wicked conceals violence" (10:11). "On the lips of the discerning, wisdom is found" (v. 13). "But with the mouth of the foolish, ruin is at hand" (v. 14). "He who conceals hatred has lying lips, and he who spreads slander is a fool" (v. 18). "When there are many words, transgression is unavoidable, but he who restrains his lips is wise. The tongue of the righteous is as choice silver, the heart of the wicked is worth little. The lips of the righteous feed many, but fools die for lack of understanding" (vv. 19–21). "The mouth of the righteous flows with wisdom, but the perverted tongue will be cut out" (v. 31). And "the lips of the righteous bring forth what is acceptable, but the mouth of the wicked what is perverted" (v. 32).

Still, the very worst kind of perverted speech is a lie. Proverbs 6:16–19 says, "There are six things which the LORD hates, yes, seven which are an abomination to Him: haughty eyes, *a lying tongue,* and hands that shed innocent blood, a heart that devises wicked plans, feet that run rapidly to evil, *a false witness who utters lies,* and one who spreads strife among brothers." Out of the seven only one is repeated: *lying.*

People who love God love truth, because God is truth. "God...cannot lie" (Titus 1:2). He is the embodiment of all that is true, and "He cannot deny Himself" (2 Timothy 2:13). People who love His Word love truth, because His Word is truth (John 17:17). People who love Christ love truth, because He is the truth (14:6). Lying lips show disdain for God.

Proverbs 29:12 says, "If a ruler pays attention to falsehood, all his ministers become wicked." If you have a liar in charge as a ruler, honest people abandon him, and he is left with the liars. Proverbs 13:5 says that this is so because a righteous man hates lying. And Proverbs 17:7 goes so far as to say lying lips are not fitting for a ruler. Lying rulers lie to abuse people for their own gain and power.

Proverbs 26:28 states, "A lying tongue hates those it crushes." When someone lies to you, they are not only abusing you but also attempting to crush you. There's a powerful illustration of this in Jeremiah 5. Jeremiah prophesied in Judah prior to the Babylonian Captivity, and he warned about the impending destruction of Jerusalem and the deportation of the Jewish people to Babylon. He faithfully proclaimed this judgment for years, weeping as he proclaimed it. He lived to see the prophecy fulfilled, and was even taken to Babylon himself.

Jeremiah 5 begins with God commanding the prophet to search the streets of Jerusalem for a man who practices justice and seeks truth. If just one such person exists, God promises to pardon the city. Isn't that astonishing? Before bringing Israel into the Babylonian captivity for seventy years, inflicting severe judgment on the Jewish people, God offered mercy if just one person who was truthful could be found.

Jeremiah writes, "O LORD, do not Your eyes look for truth? You have smitten them, but they did not weaken; You have consumed them, but they refused to take correction. They have made their faces harder than rock; they have refused to repent" (v. 3). Despite experiencing divine discipline, the people remained unrepentant and hardhearted. They stubbornly refused to acknowledge their sinful lies.

Lying is such a deadly sin because it invariably spawns worse evils. Liars are capable of any crime, so skilled are they at concealing their sins. Habitual lying removes any sense of moral boundaries. When someone is comfortable with lying, no moral restraint can contain his evil appetites.

Conversely, those committed to truthfulness *must* avoid sins that require deception.

Teach your children the value of truthfulness. By instilling in them a sense of responsibility for speaking the truth, you provide a safeguard against their susceptibility to all kinds of temptation. They will find it hard to sin and then lie about it if they have been raised to prioritize truthfulness.

In Jeremiah's time, people had grown so accustomed to swearing falsely that promises were routinely considered untrustworthy. People had become skilled liars, and the long-term result was an evil culture that seemed to reward sly deception in people's business dealings and elsewhere. Jeremiah observed the wickedness of that behavior and assumed people were merely ignorant of God's ways. He wrote, "Then I said, 'They are only the poor, they are foolish; for they do not know the way of the LORD or the ordinance of their God. I will go to the great and will speak to them, for they know the way of the LORD or the ordinance of their God'" (Jeremiah 5:4–5).

He ultimately found, however, that even the people who should have known better had abandoned the truth—including the religious leaders, civic officials, and supposedly devout people in Israel. "They too, with one accord, have broken the yoke and burst the bonds" (v. 5). There was no one in that culture who valued honesty anymore.

Even worse transgressions and apostasies had accumulated because the people grew comfortable with lying. They did not care for truth, so they had no compunctions about engaging in any kind of wrongdoing they could cover with a lie. They broke their oaths, they were unfaithful to their marriage partners, and they sinned directly against their God. By forsaking truthfulness before God, they ushered their own sons and daughters into spiritual self-destruction. In verse 7, God asks them, "Why should I pardon you? Your sons have forsaken Me and sworn by those who are not gods." They committed sexual sin, too: "They committed adultery and trooped to the harlot's house" (v. 7). Liars corrupt every aspect of life.

But a lack of honesty is especially destructive in the heart and mind of a child. Pathological liars are usually people who developed that pathology in childhood. As the passage in Jeremiah 5 illustrates, parents who model dishonesty wreak spiritual destruction in the hearts of their children. As we also see in that passage, the person who is comfortable with dishonesty has destroyed the normal restraints of conscience and simple propriety. The child who grows up thinking dishonesty is normal and acceptable will himself be capable of any crime.

So parents: If you want to win one of the most important battles in the war against children, make your home and family a place where truth is honored and lies are not tolerated.

# CHAPTER FIVE

# THE WAR IS NOT AGAINST FLESH AND BLOOD

The war on children is raging in education, entertainment, psychology, politics, and practically every other earthly realm where parents or children can be influenced. But it is not just an earthly battle; it extends far beyond all those domains. Indeed, as we noted in chapter 2, this is not a carnal battle. It is chiefly a *spiritual* conflict, with the devil himself as commander in chief of the incursion. In other words, the conflict we are concerned with is a vast, far-reaching *satanic* assault on children.

The war on children is not an armed conflict, and it will not be won with literal military might or human strength. As Ephesians 6:12 says, "Our struggle is not against flesh and blood, but against the rulers, against the powers, against the world forces of this darkness, against the spiritual forces of wickedness in the heavenly places." Our ultimate adversaries are not people, but demonic forces peddling unbiblical ideas and false belief systems.

That is why "the weapons of our warfare are not of the flesh" (2 Corinthians 10:4). Earthly firepower is no good against an adversary who is waging war by spreading falsehoods. But to be clear, the war on children won't be won with *any* kind of fleshly weaponry. That includes human philosophy, earthly politics, boycotts, demonstrations, mass rallies, and all similar strategies. Such tactics cannot ultimately defeat the lies of Satan and his minions. Those are not necessarily bad undertakings, and some of them might even do a limited amount of temporary good. However, the most important duty for Christians in this war is to answer devilish lies with God's truth. That means our most essential (and most effective) strategy for winning this war is to declare the Word of God, live by it, and teach it diligently to our own children.

Meanwhile, we must never allow our own personal preferences, polemical devices, or a concern for political correctness to eclipse the truth of God's Word. We must be clear and relentless in proclaiming the gospel message in particular, because gospel truth is the complete and decisive answer to Satan and his lies. The gospel is also the one true and permanent remedy for human hearts that are by nature hostile to God. Paul declares, "I am not ashamed of the gospel, for it is the power of God for salvation to everyone who believes" (Romans 1:16).

The devil's war against children assumes various forms, but currently, the chief battleground is a culture that is increasingly hostile to truth. During the post-Enlightenment and post-Reformation eras, *modernism* mounted a secular attack on biblical principles. The basic modernist notion was that science is a more reliable test of truth than Scripture. Still, modernists believed the pursuit of truth was paramount.

We now live in the *postmodern* era, where the dominant idea is that if any absolute or universal truth exists, it cannot be objectively known with any degree of certainty. "Truth," therefore, is always a matter of one's personal perspective. That is why people commonly speak of "my truth" and "your truth." The prevailing concept is that "truth" is whatever fits each individual's own judgment and preferences. Truth itself has become malleable. If you believe you were born in a body that doesn't match your gender, your belief (rather than any objective fact) is supposed to determine what's true and valid—even if it's "valid" only for you.

With such a twisted perspective of truth, children today are relentlessly encouraged to discover (or simply imagine and invent) whatever they want to be true.

As a result, we have transitioned into a culture that actively promotes falsehoods and demands acceptance of what is obviously *not* true, undermining the very concept of truth. It is an all-out assault on truth and a deliberate rejection of reality.

Children are suffering the most significant consequences in this battle, because those perpetrating postmodern attitudes about truth and reality are targeting the youngest people. The assault starts in early childhood, where it is carried out through education and the media. We cannot passively rely on the public educational system, social structures, politics, electronic devices, the medical establishment, or the entertainment media to teach children truth. In fact, all of these have been used for the propagation of lies. In essence, Bible-believing people are left without support in a society wholly devoted to anti-truth and satanic paganism. Consequently, the profound responsibility of our stewardship as parents is a matter of the utmost urgency.

In spite of the challenges, Proverbs 13:22 says, "A good man leaves an inheritance to his children's children." That text is not only about material prosperity and the financial wealth that is accumulated and passed on from generation to generation. It does have the generational transfer of wealth chiefly in view, but the underlying principle also has implications for the impact that a virtuous life and a legacy of truthfulness can have for one's offspring.

As we have seen, evil people leave a lasting impact on future generations because the sins of the fathers affect their children and grandchildren to the third and fourth generations (Exodus 34:7). But likewise, those who diligently follow, obey, and teach their children the truth of God's Word leave an invaluable *spiritual* inheritance to subsequent generations.

With that idea in focus, look once more at the biblical foundation of all instructions on parenting. This is where we began, so it's fitting that we should return there—Deuteronomy 6:4–9:

> Hear, O Israel! The LORD is our God, the LORD is one! You shall love the LORD your God with all your heart and with all your soul and with all your might. These words, which I am commanding you today, shall be on your heart. You shall teach them diligently to your sons and shall talk of them when you sit in your house and when you walk by the way and when you lie down and when you rise up. You shall bind them as a sign on your hand and they shall be as frontals on your forehead. You shall write them on the doorposts of your house and on your gates.

There, again, lies the sum of all biblical instructions for parents. That passage frames our responsibility to the children God entrusts to us.

Obviously, all parents have a duty to protect their children's lives. Beyond that—and this is where the parent's most important stewardship begins—we have a sacred responsibility to teach our children to love the Lord their God with all their being.

The New Testament parallel to Deuteronomy 6 is that single verse that we have also examined already—Ephesians 6:4: "Fathers [Greek, *pateres*; sometimes translated "parents"], do not provoke your children to anger, but bring them up in the discipline and instruction of the Lord." "Bring[ing] them up" is every parent's duty. Children will not raise themselves properly. Proverbs 29:15 says, "A child who gets his own way brings shame to his mother." That is the inevitable outcome when parents neglect their responsibility.

So, as we have seen from the beginning, proper biblical parenting requires relentless effort, and the ultimate goal is to raise our children to love God with all their hearts. Parenting is not about modifying behavior or seeking external conformity in the child. Any wise, biblically-minded parent will always address the child's heart. Indeed, the principle given in Proverbs 4:23 is vital: "Watch over your heart with all diligence, for from it flow the springs of life." In short, guarding the child's heart—and teaching our children to guard their own hearts—is the weightiest responsibility in the task of parenting.

Allow me to introduce you to your child's heart. In Mark 7:20, Jesus declares, "That which proceeds out of the man, that is what defiles the man." You must understand this: There are only two possibilities. Either the troubled state of any fallen sinner is a result of external forces acting upon him, or the troubled state of the sinner is a reflection of something wrong *within* him. The prevailing culture likes to attribute all our problems to oppression, inequity, trauma, a poor self-image, systemic injustice, or some similar external cause. The Bible, however, teaches clearly that the root of the human problem lies within our own hearts.

Jesus' full statement makes His meaning clear and inescapable. We are not ultimately *victims* of sin. When we are guilty of moral failure or when sin has left us spiritually defiled, it is never because some evil or pollution has assaulted us from outside our own hearts. No—

> That which proceeds out of the man, that is what defiles the man. For from within, out of the heart of men, proceed the evil thoughts, fornications, thefts, murders, adulteries, deeds of coveting and wickedness, as well as deceit, sensuality, envy, slander, pride and foolishness. All these evil things proceed from within and defile the man. (Mark 7:20–23)

Everything currently dismantling our culture and wrecking the lives of people we know is an expression of the wickedness that lies inside every fallen human heart. That includes riots, sexual immorality, every evil act, every wrong ideology, and whatever other social evils people try to blame on injustice or oppression. All the evil in those troubles comes "from within, out of the heart of men."

What is needed, then, is the transformation of a fallen heart, and that is accomplished *only* through the gospel. In Jesus' words, sinners "must be born again" (John 3:7), for "unless one is born again he cannot see the kingdom of God" (v. 3).

We cannot attribute crimes and wickedness to external circumstances beyond the sinner's control. Human evil stems from human corruption—and that is a universal problem. "For all have sinned and fall short of the glory of God" (Romans 3:23).

It is truly remarkable that we do not harm each other more frequently. The question is: How is it possible for so many people to live together for extended periods without resorting to violence? The answer is that God's common grace and goodness restrain the full expression of human evil. He has given us a conscience, our parents, government authority, and the presence of the church, and all of these serve as deterrents to the evils we are capable of. After all, the fundamental nature of fallen humanity tends toward hate, selfishness, pride, and falsehood. "As it is written, 'There is none righteous, not even one'" (Romans 3:10). Make no mistake, apart from God's grace, we are all capable of wickedness as dark as the deeds of any serial killer or genocidal dictator.

Furthermore, when true religion is abandoned, something metaphysical must take its place. Wherever sound biblical influences are eliminated, some replacement religion will be invented, and it will align with the prevailing culture. In this culture of love for hatred, movements ranging from white supremacy to Critical Race Theory emerge—promoting a plethora of false ideologies including feminism, Marxism, scientism, wokism, and anarchy. These serve as religious belief systems suited for a secular society. They are faith-based dogmas that require unquestioning acceptance, and they become the lens through which every other idea is seen, and the standard by which every truth-claim is judged.

The notion that our problems are all caused by other people and circumstances around us fails to address the core issue. Our most basic problems stem from within ourselves, because of our inherent and natural wickedness and our natural inclination toward sin.

Remember that Jesus said the foremost commandment is to love God, and the second in order of priority is to love our neighbors (Mark 12:29–31). Both of these commands apply to what is in our hearts, not merely how we act. Given that fact, parents must acknowledge that behavior should not be our only concern as we approach the task of raising our children. Teaching them good and righteous behavior is certainly *part* of our responsibility—but it is not the primary or ultimate goal. You may achieve the temporary appearance of success if all you do is control your children's actions, but unless their hearts are inclined to God, they will inevitably return to the default state of human fallenness.

Modern society is heavily invested in teaching children to rebel against virtue and authority. But aside from Solomon's instructions to his son in Proverbs, the Bible addresses only one commandment directly to children, and that one imperative is repeated twice: "Children, obey your parents in the Lord, for this is right" (Ephesians 6:1); and, "Children, be obedient to your parents in all things, for this is well-pleasing to the Lord" (Colossians 3:20). Satan, however, has deceived entire generations of foolish young people into believing that rebellion against their parents, rejection of God, and resistance to His Words are noble pursuits. That is the fruit of our culture's reversion to paganism.

Rebellion is not something anyone should teach children. Any belief system that exalts rebellion, resentment, and hatred as noble is destructive. That's why it is so disheartening when evangelical leaders lend credence to ideologies like Critical Race Theory or try to stir sympathy for mass movements that promote anarchy or insurrection. These, again, are false, anti-Christian religions that purposely foment bitterness and revolt.

As parents diligently raising your children, you must address four areas of their development. Luke 2:52 records that Jesus increased "in wisdom and stature, and in favor with God and men." That statement encompasses intellectual, physical, spiritual, and social growth.

All four of those categories are addressed in various ways in the book of Proverbs. Because Proverbs is so full of wisdom for both parents and children, it's worth another look.

The key word associated with Solomon's name—and one of his principle concerns as a father—is *wisdom*. The wisdom Solomon has in mind is heavily weighted with the concept of *discernment*—which Solomon himself might define as skill in distinguishing truth from falsehood; an ability to make prudent decisions rather than foolish ones; devotion to godliness and an aversion to wickedness; skill in dealing with other people; and a habit of self-control. That covers all the categories of intellectual, physical, spiritual, and social growth—"wisdom...stature...favor with God and men."

Proverbs 3:13–18 says,

> How blessed is the man who finds wisdom and the man who gains understanding. For her profit is better than the profit of silver and her gain better than fine gold. She is more precious than jewels; and nothing you desire compares with her. Long life is in her right hand; in her left hand are riches and honor. Her ways are pleasant ways and all her paths are peace. She is a tree of life to those who take hold of her, and happy are all who hold her fast.

Proverbs 23:23 says, "Buy truth, and do not sell it, get wisdom and instruction and understanding."

In Proverbs 4:5, a father implores his son, saying, "Acquire wisdom! Acquire understanding! Do not forget nor turn away from the words of my mouth." The father's greatest desire for his son is that he be wise rather than foolish. That is the driving motive for healthy parenting. The father continues:

> Do not forsake her, and she will guard you; love her, and she will watch over you. The beginning of wisdom is: Acquire wisdom; and with all your acquiring, get understanding. Prize her, and she will exalt you; she will honor you if you embrace

her. She will place on your head a garland of grace; she will present you with a crown of beauty. (vv. 6–9)

He goes on to urge his son to listen to and accept his teachings because (as the promise attached to the fifth commandment suggests) that will lead to a long and prosperous life: "Hear, my son, and accept my sayings and the years of your life will be many. I have directed you in the way of wisdom; I have led you in upright paths. When you walk, your steps will not be impeded; and if you run, you will not stumble" (Proverbs 4:10–12).

How, exactly, is the wisdom of discernment described in Proverbs acquired? We have already established that it starts with the fear of God (Proverbs 9:10). Again, the true fear of God is a broad category encompassing a range of attitudes, from profound love to reverential awe—and even a sense of dread. Once more: "It is a terrifying thing to fall into the hands of the living God" (Hebrews 10:31). As we noted many pages ago, a healthy fear of God involves a deep understanding of God's attributes—with a conscious recognition of His authority and power. He is the One who judges righteously, and He can destroy both body and soul in hell.

Rejecting the fear of the true and living God revealed in Scripture will hinder the acquisition of wisdom. Without the true fear of God, humans have no internal restraint for mitigating their own wickedness. The person who simply does not fear God will inflict harm and destruction upon others, and constantly attempt to suppress their innate sense of accountability to God and the basic moral precepts He has written in their hearts (Romans 2:14–15). That is a recipe for unbridled depravity.

In the previous chapter we also stressed the critical importance of parents' teaching their children to speak the truth. "Put away from you a deceitful mouth and put devious speech far from you" (Proverbs 4:24). Truth is of the utmost importance—especially in an era like ours—because it serves as a protective framework for navigating a cultural landscape riddled with falsehood. Unless you value truth and function always in harmony with truth, you are in perilous danger. Your children are walking through a cultural minefield if they don't have the discernment to understand the truth.

A third theme that must be conveyed to children is the importance of guarding their minds. Proverbs 3:3 advises, "Do not let kindness and truth leave you; bind them around your neck, write them on the tablet of your heart." This is of course the very principle spelled out expressly in Proverbs 4:23: "Watch over your heart with all diligence, for from it flow the springs of life." The "heart" in most biblical contexts speaks of the mind, the imagination, the part of every human creature where our thoughts and beliefs and rational powers reside. It is the source of everything we do, say, or think, and if it is poisoned with iniquity or falsehood, that will affect all the rest of life.

So Scripture stresses—not just in Proverbs 4:23, but in a host of texts—to guard what we think about; keep a watch on our *minds*. "Give heed to yourself and keep your soul diligently" (Deuteronomy 4:9). "Keep watching and praying that you may not come into temptation; the spirit is willing, but the flesh is weak" (Mark 14:38). "As he thinks within himself, so he is" (Proverbs 23:7)—or, "As he calculates in his soul, so he is" (LSB). Everything that shapes our beliefs and our actions comes from the heart—and specifically, from the mind. Therefore, "be transformed by the renewing of your mind, so that you may prove what the will of God is" (Romans 12:2). Guarding the mind and maintaining a virtuous thought life is essential, as all our actions flow from our thoughts.

In Matthew 12:33–35 Jesus, speaking to some leading Pharisees, said, "Either make the tree good and its fruit good, or make the tree bad and its fruit bad; for the tree is known by its fruit. You brood of vipers, how can you, being evil, speak what is good? For the mouth speaks out of that which fills the heart. The good man brings out of his good treasure what is good; and the evil man brings out of his evil treasure what is evil."

That indictment was profound. He expressly calls them the "brood [offspring] of vipers...evil," even though they were the most fastidious religious devotees—the strictest pietists—of that era. He was implying that by listening to their words and observing their actions, one could discern the real condition of their hearts, because the wickedness they were trying so diligently to cover with their hypocrisy was still manifest in their actions and speech. They were living examples of why behavior modification is not the endgame in parenting. Parents must address the issues of our children's hearts, not just behavior, or else we are raising hypocrites.

There is significant instruction at the beginning of the Psalms that all parents must carefully consider before sending their young ones off to school where they may be defenseless against the harmful strategies of those who are more intellectually adept. Psalm 1 says, "How blessed is the man who does not walk in the counsel of the wicked, nor stand in the path of sinners, nor sit in the seat of scoffers!" It is dangerous to associate with the wicked, let alone to engage in prolonged exposure to their ideologies. Why would a Christian choose to sit in the classroom of a mocker and be lectured by someone who serves as an agent of Satan, seeking to destroy their eternal soul? Fathers and mothers are supposed to be the guardians of their children's minds.

So fear your God. Speak the truth. Guard your mind. Furthermore, *choose your companions wisely*. Do not allow them to choose you; you must make the selection. Proverbs 1:10 says, "My son, if sinners entice you, do not consent." Evildoers are skilled at enticing naive people to join them in acts of wickedness. Train your children to resist. The passage continues with a warning:

> If they say, "Come with us, let us lie in wait for blood, let us ambush the innocent without cause; let us swallow them alive like Sheol, even whole, as those who go down to the pit; we will find all kinds of precious wealth, we will fill our houses with spoil; throw in your lot with us, we shall all have one purse," my son, do not walk in the way with them. Keep your feet from their path, for their feet run to evil and they hasten to shed blood. Indeed, it is useless to spread the baited net in the sight of any bird; but they lie in wait for their own blood; they ambush their own lives. So are the ways of everyone who gains by violence; it takes away the life of its possessors. (vv. 11–19)

One chapter later, Proverbs 2:11–15 says,

> Discretion will guard you, understanding will watch over you, to deliver you from the way of evil, from the man who speaks perverse things; from those who leave the paths of uprightness to walk in the ways of darkness; who delight in doing evil and rejoice in the perversity of evil; whose paths are crooked, and who are devious in their ways.

The book of Proverbs continues to caution repeatedly against being enticed by the strange woman and the adulteress who uses flattery. Only by walking in the way of the righteous and staying on the path of the upright can a person remain blameless. You *must* teach your children not to be seduced by those who engage in evil, whether in the real world or the virtual realm of the Internet.

The promise of a fulfilled life is woven through all the principles of wisdom. Revisiting Proverbs 4:10–18 yields another admonition to stay away from the path of the wicked. Here Solomon's words of caution are reinforced with some key life lessons about the consequences of such folly:

> Hear, my son, and accept my sayings and the years of your life will be many. I have directed you in the way of wisdom; I have led you in upright paths. When you walk, your steps will not be impeded; and if you run, you will not stumble. Take hold of instruction; do not let go. Guard her, for she is your life. *Do not enter the path of the wicked and do not proceed in the way of evil men. Avoid it, do not pass by it; turn away from it and pass on.* For they cannot sleep unless they do evil; and they are robbed of sleep unless they make someone stumble. For they eat the bread of wickedness and drink the wine of violence. But the path of the righteous is like the light of dawn, that shines brighter and brighter until the full day.

So it is crucial to follow the righteous path, since the way of the wicked is spiritual darkness.

Proverbs 18:24 adds, "A man of too many friends comes to ruin." Why? And shouldn't we strive for as many friends as possible? The key to that statement is the Hebrew word for "friends." It's the word *rea*, which means "fellow" or "associate." In other words, being overly welcoming and having an excessive number of partnerships with people of bad moral persuasions can lead to ruin.

The second half of that Proverb says, "But there is a friend who sticks closer than a brother." In other words, a true friend is committed to your welfare; he is not seeking an alliance with you for what he can get out of it for himself. It is better to have a few close, loving friends who are connected by genuine love and who are honest, loyal, virtuous, kind, and committed to the path of truth and righteousness—rather than a vast web of partnerships with people motivated to use you for their own advantage and influence you for evil.

Let me add one more point. Teach your children to fear God, speak the truth, guard their minds, choose their companions wisely, *and exercise control over their desires.*

Proverbs 5:21–23 once more gives an important lesson about controlling one's own desires: "The ways of a man are before the eyes of the LORD, and He watches all his paths. His own iniquities will capture the wicked, and he will be held with the cords of his sin. He will die for lack of instruction, and in the greatness of his folly he will go astray."

That is a wise warning that evil desire will imprison and trap individuals in sin. Evil desire comes in various forms. It's why the young man struggling with lust needs to be delivered from the influence of a seductive and adulterous woman who uses flattery (2:16). It's why postmodern "sex education" is so damaging to young children, and instead, they need to learn the importance of sexual purity and self-control. It is your task as a parent to make sure they get that training.

Sexual immorality stemming from uncontrolled lust has been the downfall of more young people than we could possibly count. "Each one is tempted when he is carried away and enticed by his own lust. Then when lust has conceived, it gives birth to sin; and when sin is accomplished, it brings forth death" (James 1:14–15). Solomon himself squandered years of potential because he gave into his own carnal lusts. The warning on Proverbs 5:3–8 applies to every kind of sexual promiscuity:

> For the lips of an adulteress drip honey and smoother than oil
> is her speech; but in the end she is bitter as wormwood, sharp
> as a two-edged sword. Her feet go down to death, her steps
> take hold of Sheol. She does not ponder the path of life; her
> ways are unstable, she does not know it.
>
> Now then, my sons, listen to me and do not depart from the
> words of my mouth. Keep your way far from her and do not go
> near the door of her house.

Verses 12–14 then lament the consequence of despising instruction and rejecting reproof: "You say, 'How I have hated instruction! And my heart spurned reproof! I have not listened to the voice of my teachers, nor inclined my ear to my instructors! I was almost in utter ruin in the midst of the assembly and congregation.'"

Proverbs 6:20–23 sounds the same note as that one simple command to children given in Colossians 3:20 and Ephesians 6:1. Solomon expands on the plea:

> My son, observe the commandment of your father and do not
> forsake the teaching of your mother; bind them continually
> on your heart; tie them around your neck. When you walk
> about, they will guide you; when you sleep, they will watch
> over you; and when you awake, they will talk to you. For the
> commandment is a lamp and the teaching is light; and reproofs
> for discipline are the way of life.

But in this context, he specifically has the issue of sexual purity in view, because he returns immediately to the importance of fleeing from the influence of an evil woman and her smooth words. He explains that the intent of his instruction is—

to keep you from the evil woman, from the smooth tongue of the adulteress. Do not desire her beauty in your heart, nor let her capture you with her eyelids. For on account of a harlot one is reduced to a loaf of bread, and an adulteress hunts for the precious life. Can a man take fire in his bosom and his clothes not be burned? Or can a man walk on hot coals and his feet not be scorched? So is the one who goes in to his neighbor's wife; whoever touches her will not go unpunished.... The one who commits adultery with a woman is lacking sense; he who would destroy himself does it. Wounds and disgrace he will find, and his reproach will not be blotted out. (Proverbs 6:24–29, 32–33)

It seems at the moment that public schools are determined to teach schoolchildren that every kind of sexual deviancy is acceptable, and they must never feel guilty or be ashamed of any kind of carnal lust. But according to Scripture, children need to be taught that every kind of sexual sin is a particularly deadly path to tread: "Flee immorality. Every other sin that a man commits is outside the body, but the immoral man sins against his own body" (1 Corinthians 6:18).

The warning against sexual sin continues throughout Proverbs. It is the overarching theme of the entire seventh chapter. Whoever pursues such sin is marching himself into disaster "as an ox goes to the slaughter" (Proverbs 7:22).

The sage closes chapter 7 with another appeal to his children— this one specifically dealing with his warnings against sexual sin: "Now therefore, my sons, listen to me, and pay attention to the words of my mouth" (v. 24). Every wise father will warn his children about the viciously destructive nature of lustful behavior.

All these lessons from the book of Proverbs are invaluable instructions for parents: Fear your God, speak the truth, guard your mind, select your companions, control your desires. Study the book of Proverbs for yourself, and you will discover that there are many more.

For example, in chapter 6 Solomon encourages wise children to pursue work. Chapter 3 mentions the wise management of money. Proverbs is a veritable manual of similar lessons for parents to teach their children. Parents need to study the wisdom of Proverbs diligently. The quest for sanctified wisdom is a lifetime pursuit.

To summarize: Failing to teach your child to fear God allows the devil to instill hatred for God. Neglecting to instruct your children in guarding their minds leads to an open-mindedness that the devil will exploit. Failing to teach obedience invites the devil to stir up rebellion. Overlooking the importance of selecting good companions exposes a child to the devil's evil influences. Neglecting to teach control over desires invites the devil to capitalize on their lust. Neglecting to teach them to watch their words and speak the truth allows the devil to make them liars. Failing to teach your son to pursue work diligently allows the devil to make him a lazy tool of hell.

In spite of sin and Satan, faithful parents who follow heaven's instructions can fulfill their responsibilities and enjoy the blessing of mature, wise children. Proverbs 22:6 affirms this: "Train up a child in the way he should go, even when he is old he will not depart from it." Victory in the war on children is offered to parents who raise their children to love God, know His truth and obey it, and stand strong against the destructive and deceitful weapons of the world.

# THE KEY BATTLEFRONTS

# CHAPTER SIX

# THE ATTACK ON CONCEPTION

The current attacks on marriage, family, and children did not arise spontaneously from nothing. The radicalism now transforming Western culture was already percolating in the secular academic world before the twentieth century even began. Marxism, feminism, Freudianism, existentialism, and a host of other radical modernist doctrines were busily planting seeds of conflict. The chief hallmark of all modernism was a rejection of biblical authority—so naturally, modernist movements typically spurned biblical morality as well.

Marxism and Communism quickly gained influence in Eastern Europe and China, and heavily oppressive communist regimes were the almost immediate result. In the West, however, where biblical Christianity still had a stronger influence in shaping people's beliefs, modernist ideas gained influence more slowly. But committed modernists relentlessly proselytized young people and students in Western universities, mainly through subtle strategies of quiet indoctrination, ideological vandalism, and intellectual sabotage.

The success of that cunning campaign became obvious with the baby-boom generation (people born in the two decades following the end of World War II). By the end of the 1960s, as the oldest baby boomers were entering adulthood, it was obvious that a seismic cultural shift was well underway. Student strikes, antiwar protests, and political upheaval seemed ubiquitous. The divorce rate was climbing; moral values were being openly discarded. Hippies were the icons of that era, advocating free love, psychedelic drugs, communal living, totally unrestrained self-expression—along with a political point of view that was dominated by Marxist and radical left-wing values.

Virtually all the distinctive political doctrines that grew out of the rebellious 1960s are hostile to biblical values and the flourishing of families and children. These include the forced redistribution of wealth by government; the welfare state; government control of utilities, transportation, healthcare, education, and social services; the elimination of gender distinctions; and the normalization of sexual deviancy. All of these policies either undermine moral convictions or make people helplessly dependent on centralized, bureaucratic government agencies for things that people have historically depended on the family to provide.

Families are commonly seen as optional. Worse yet, television sitcoms, popular literature, popular psychology, and official government propaganda frequently portray the family as an impediment to one's personal comfort and a happy life. Government is the one source people are encouraged to look to for any help they might need.

But with all those factors tearing at the fabric of families, it was a major court decision in 1973 that served as both a formal declaration of open hostilities and an opening salvo—a preemptive strike—in the war on children. It was the United States Supreme Court ruling in the case of Roe v. Wade, a decision that in effect legalized and normalized abortion on demand. In practice, that ruling literally ended the very existence of millions of children.

Roe v. Wade was a turning point and a catalyst for additional assaults on children, nuclear families, parenthood, and morality.

The long-term damaging effects of all those worldview changes, together with the abortion epidemic, have been profound and multifarious. But perhaps the most reprehensible and malignant result of this massive cultural shift is the way it has fostered a widespread belief that it's better for people not to have children at all. Children are deemed an inconvenience—or worse, a threat to the environment, an evil more than a blessing.

An online platform recently ran a feminist article titled, "What Would the World Look Like If NOT Having Kids Was the Cultural Norm?"[13] The subtitle purported to answer the question: "Less stress, less heartache, less judgment." Deliberate childlessness has become far more of a cultural norm than it has ever been, and that is not a positive trend for the human race.

Here are some facts: People around the world are having fewer children—significantly fewer. In 2020, the BBC reported that falling fertility rates could dramatically decrease the global population by the end of the century.[14] Citing a study from the University of Washington's Institute for Health Metrics and Evaluation, the article notes that the average woman in 1950 gave birth to 4.7 children over the course of her life. By 2017, that number had been cut nearly in half, with the global average sitting at just 2.4.

That sharp decline in conception could lead to catastrophic results in the decades ahead. On the current trajectory, it is estimated that Japan could see its population fall from 128 million in 2017 to fewer than 53 million by 2100. Italy could likewise drop from 61 million to just 28 million over the same span. Altogether, more than twenty countries could lose at least half their population in the next eighty years.[15]

Predictions for the United States aren't quite that dire, but national fertility rates are nevertheless at an all-time low. The numbers have actually been on the decline for years. In 2018, the US total fertility rate (an estimate of how many children a woman will give birth to in her lifetime, based on current fertility patterns) fell to 1.73, surpassing a previous low from the 1970s.[16] But according to the National Center for Health Statistics, that number plummeted in 2020 to just 1.64[17]—well below the 2.08 "replacement level" fertility required to maintain population numbers.[18]

Given the global decline, one might assume there could be environmental or physiological factors in play. But one recent survey shows that it's simply a choice, with 44 percent of non-parent adults saying it is unlikely they will ever have children.[19]

How do we make sense of the precipitous drop in conception? Why have so many young people grown disillusioned and uninterested in having children? After all, God's first command to the human race was simple and straightforward: "Be fruitful and multiply, and fill the earth, and subdue it; and rule over the fish of the sea and over the birds of the sky and over every living thing that moves on the earth" (Genesis 1:28).

So the disparagement of parenthood is a direct assault against God's original mandate to our first parents—and this is without a doubt, one of the more calamitous results stemming from the breakdown of the family and our culture's rejection of family values. The rising frequency of divorce, rampant sexual sin, the feminist attack on motherhood, and upended gender roles are all sinful trends, and they all play a part in the birthrate decline. In other words, the attack on conception is inextricably linked to the assault on the family that we have been talking about throughout this book. And we will have more to say about that shortly.

But before we delve even deeper into that subject, let's acknowledge that the reasons behind this global decline in conception and childbirth run deeper than just the satanic perversion of God's design for marriage and the family. In fact, the problem begins with individuals.

It starts with an epidemic of adolescence, as young men and women today are taking much longer to grow up—if they ever do. It's not a question of how quickly a young person can move out and start a family of his own. Instead, it's how long he can keep living under his parents' roof, how long he can stay on his parents' insurance, and how long he can hold off the responsibilities of adulthood. Those are admitted goals of countless young people today—not just adolescents, but twenty- and thirty-somethings as well.[20]

Frankly, our culture has done everything possible to dissuade young people from growing up. Bombarded with constant entertainment and distraction, many have given no thought to the kind of life they want or how to pursue it. The value of hard work and dedication is a foreign concept, as young people drift through life along the path of least resistance.

Some are deceived by the illusory world of social media and obsessed with delusions of grandeur. They see fame as a worthwhile pursuit, regardless of how it's achieved. Soon their whole lives are swallowed up in self-promotion, as they strive endlessly for more attention and influence. They've made idols of themselves, and spend their lives in dedicated service to their own insatiable self-gratification and self-promotion.

Put yourself in that mindset for a moment. If your life were devoted to your own satisfaction and the pursuit of your goals—to the exclusion of all else—*of course* you would see children as a hindrance, an interruption, and an unwanted distraction. Why would you want to pour years of your life and untold resources into feeding, clothing, housing, and raising another person? That's just throwing away time and money that could otherwise be spent on yourself.

Moreover, this self-involved generation suffers from severe emotional immaturity. They can't control their emotions. Too often, their emotions have control over them. We're now surrounded by young people who have failed to develop any capacity for careful, critical thought. They can only emote.

These unrestrained emotions have led to a culture dominated by anger and outrage. It is 2023 as I write this. Over the past decade, a series of "social justice" movements endorsed and encouraged by the media have collectively been tearing the fabric of our culture to shreds—undermining civility, fomenting ethnic hostilities, openly flouting laws, and literally seeking to dismantle any beliefs or institutions that their parents and grandparents affirmed or treasured. They have shown a particular hostility to *biblical* values. They routinely employ unbridled anger like a wrecking ball in this foolhardy demolition project. Occupy Wall Street, Black Lives Matter, Antifa, the infamous (and ultimately deadly) CHOP/CHAZ movement in Seattle, climate change activists, along with countless other ad hoc protest groups have all leveraged emotion over information to exert their influence for the ruination of any spiritually healthy and well-ordered way of life. That's not progress or social reform. It's a jealous tantrum.

As outrage culture has increasingly come to dominate society, it has pushed aside the shared moral and social values that once formed the foundation for relationships and marriages. They have been replaced by unhinged emotions. For many today, their worldview boils down to what they're agitated and angry about. While young people might share those passions with others for a time, those fleeting feelings are no basis for a lasting relationship, much less a family. And when your life is devoted to expressing your outrage and venting bile, there's no time or energy left for nurturing and raising a child.

There's another factor to consider when it comes to declining populations. On top of the selfishness and emotional immaturity of recent generations, we also need to recognize the relative cheapness of human life. Social media has turned our fellow man into little more than a digital avatar. No longer do we recognize the unique dignity of mankind, or the likeness of God in other people.

And with nothing to set humans apart from any other created being, the question for many quickly becomes, *Why bother having a child when I could just get a dog?*

The phenomenon of people viewing pets as acceptable proxies for children is truly stunning and deeply disturbing. They dress their animals up in little outfits and push them around in strollers. One woman was recently caught attempting to breastfeed a swaddled cat on a commercial airline.[21] How did such a corrupt, confused mindset take hold in a supposedly civilized society?

What we're seeing is essentially a fulfillment of Romans 1 and Paul's description of sin's degrading effects—which are ultimately a judgment from God. The apostle writes,

> For the wrath of God is revealed from heaven against all ungodliness and unrighteousness of men who suppress the truth in unrighteousness, because that which is known about God is evident within them; for God made it evident to them. For since the creation of the world His invisible attributes, His eternal power and divine nature, have been clearly seen, being understood through what has been made, so that they are without excuse. (Romans 1:18–20)

Sinful man wants nothing to do with God; he will stop at nothing to deny his Creator's authority over him. That means he must dismiss or explain away the obvious evidence of God's work in creation.

That's how we get theories about evolution and the big bang. Sinners will seize on any explanation, no matter how improbable or illogical, if it offers them an escape from the truth of Scripture. But efforts to deny the obvious truth aren't isolated to the question of origins. Sinful man routinely denies God's sustaining work, theorizing instead that the laws binding the physical universe together somehow emerged by random chance as if magically— from sheer chaos, or from formerly inert matter. They likewise deny God's providence, preferring to chalk up any blessing, privilege, or good fortune to dumb luck.

Another way the world denies the truth about God is by ignoring His likeness in other humans. Humanity is obviously set apart from all other created beings. We have a dynamic intellect and the capacity to reason. We have a will and complex emotions. We are capable of self-reflection. We can communicate. We have an innate moral sense—we know right from wrong. We have a conscience that condemns us when we do wrong. We feel our accountability to a higher Being. And we live forever. All those characteristics and more were bestowed specifically on humans when we were made in the image of God. In the Lord's good design, we have the ability to reflect what theologians refer to as God's communicable attributes. In other words, we were "made... in the likeness of God" (Genesis 5:1).

But the world is determined to deny the uniqueness of Adam and his offspring in God's creation. Those who reject God want you to believe that man is nothing more than a highly evolved animal. In their view the differences between us and monkeys and dolphins (or chickens and worms, for that matter) are negligible. And worst of all, they want you to believe that animals are worthy of the same dignity and deference we afford to other humans.

That is the stupefying effect of sin that Paul describes in Romans 1.

> For even though they knew God, they did not honor Him as God or give thanks, but they became futile in their speculations, and their foolish heart was darkened. Professing to be wise, they became fools, and exchanged the glory of the incorruptible God for an image in the form of corruptible man and of birds and four-footed animals and crawling creatures. (vv. 21–23)

Those driving the direction of our society have "exchanged the truth of God for a lie, and worshiped and served the creature rather than the Creator" (v. 25).

That is how so many people today can believe the lie that their pets are perfectly viable replacements for children. They may not be consciously acting out of open rebellion to God and His design. They may not recognize such foolishness as defiance. But the misplaced affection they pour out on their "fur babies" is nonetheless an assault on the authority of their Creator and an insult to His likeness that He chose to uniquely display in Adam and his offspring.

Taking those factors together—the epidemic of adolescence, the dominance of outrage culture, and the widespread disrespect for God's ultimate creative work in mankind—it's no wonder that we're seeing a cultural retreat from parenting. What is somewhat surprising is that we're seeing it *in the church*.

While the drop in childbearing in the church has not been as dramatic as the global figures discussed above, it is clear that even Christians today are having fewer children than past generations.[22] And while some of the trends we've already identified could certainly be to blame for this decline, let me suggest some additional factors that I believe pose a particular threat to young believers.

In short, I'm concerned that young Christians today are buying into some of the world's most pervasive and persistent deceptions.

To begin with, young believers may be distracted from starting families by the selfish pursuit of personal happiness. Certainly, their peers in the world lead lives dominated by the endless search for satisfaction. There's always a bigger paycheck, a more prestigious job, a better car, a larger home, and a more glamorous lifestyle to achieve.

We've seen the purveyors of the prosperity gospel leverage that same insatiable pursuit of temporal satisfaction and happiness. Their deceptive doctrine has sown significant confusion in the church, with many professing believers convinced that God's primary concern is meeting their wants and needs—that Christ died to fulfill their hopes and dreams. They've succeeded in selling Satan's lie that God just wants you to be happy, legitimizing selfish lifestyles that are indistinguishable from the world. Popular megachurches force youth into superficial stimulations of shallow feelings and help to perpetuate their depthless adolescence by excluding anything that could be considered mature and intellectually challenging and enriching.

But Scripture is clear that sinners cannot satisfy their wicked appetites, that there is no lasting happiness to be found in this world. King Solomon had virtually unparalleled means to pursue every avenue of pleasure and personal gain one could imagine. His words in Ecclesiastes testify to the futility of his selfish search for satisfaction.

> I said to myself, "Come now, I will test you with pleasure. So enjoy yourself." And behold, it too was futility. I said of laughter, "It is madness," and of pleasure, "What does it accomplish?" I explored with my mind how to stimulate my body with wine while my mind was guiding me wisely, and how to take hold of folly, until I could see what good there is for the sons of men to do under heaven the few years of their lives. I enlarged my works: I built houses for myself, I planted vineyards for myself; I made gardens and parks for myself and I planted in them all kinds of fruit trees; I made ponds of water for myself from which to irrigate a forest of growing trees. I bought male and female slaves and I had homeborn slaves. Also I possessed flocks and herds larger than all who preceded me in Jerusalem. Also, I collected for myself silver and gold and the treasure of kings and provinces. I provided for myself male and female singers and the pleasures of men—many concubines.
>
> Then I became great and increased more than all who preceded me in Jerusalem. My wisdom also stood by me. All that my eyes desired I did not refuse them. I did not withhold my heart from any pleasure, for my heart was pleased because of all my labor and this was my reward for all my labor. Thus I considered all my activities which my hands had done and the labor which I had exerted, and behold all was vanity and striving after wind and there was no profit under the sun. (Ecclesiastes 2:1–11)

Solomon confesses that he devoted his life to the pursuit of pleasure, only to find that none of it mattered—that it couldn't last or satisfy. He had been "striving after the wind," which is to say he was chasing something he couldn't legitimately hope to catch. There had been no profit or lasting value in his attempts to achieve worldly happiness. In the end, it was all worthless.

God's people need to learn from Solomon's example. The worldly influences dominating our culture promote the kind of shortsighted, selfish lifestyle that he rightly identified as "vanity"—utterly useless and without any eternal value. We need to see a purpose beyond this world's passing pleasures. We need to echo Solomon's words from the end of Ecclesiastes, "The conclusion, when all has been heard, is: fear God and keep His commandments, because this applies to every person. For God will bring every act to judgment, everything which is hidden, whether it is good or evil" (Ecclesiastes 12:13–14).

The believer's life should be devoted solely to the glory of God. Our temporal happiness pales in comparison to the eternal glory of our Lord and Savior. We cannot forget that we "were bought with a price" (1 Corinthians 7:23). We were "created in Christ Jesus for good works" (Ephesians 2:10). He has called us from death to life for the work of His kingdom, not for the satisfaction of our whims. Every aspect of our lives should be devoted to His glory alone (1 Corinthians 10:31).

Moreover, we need to fix our eyes on the Lord and His heavenly kingdom. Nothing makes the passing pleasures of this world fade faster than a right view of God and the anticipation of an eternity with Him. Our citizenship is in heaven, and our hearts should be, too. We need to say with the psalmist,

Whom have I in heaven but You? And besides You, I desire nothing on earth. My flesh and my heart may fail, but God is the strength of my heart and my portion forever. For, behold, those who are far from You will perish; You have destroyed all those who are unfaithful to You. But as for me, the nearness of God is my good; I have made the Lord GOD my refuge, that I may tell of all Your works. (Psalm 73:25–28)

Don't mistake that as an argument for asceticism. We don't need to shun the rest of the world and live in dour isolation. God has filled this world with good things for our enjoyment. Indeed, Scripture says expressly that He "richly supplies us with all things to enjoy" (1 Timothy 6:17). That includes the blessings of marriage and family, with children ("the fruit of the womb") chief among them (Psalm 127:3). We need to recognize God's hand in bestowing those good gifts to us, and praise Him accordingly. As Paul wrote, "For from Him and through Him and to Him are all things. To Him be the glory forever. Amen" (Romans 11:36).

Along with the false pursuit of temporal happiness, there's another deceptive idea that might be dissuading young Christians from starting families—we can call it the security of *things*. The world finds a sense of security in the accumulation of material possessions, as though houses, cars, investment portfolios, and savings accounts can guarantee true stability amid the chaos of life.

Christians are susceptible to the lie that what you own has lasting value. Some give in to the temptations of worldly materialism and greed. Others might simply give too much credence to the belief that they need certain things or a specific amount of money to feel secure, putting the rest of life on hold until they've reached those thresholds.

But in reality, the things we own don't provide any true security or stability. In fact, the more we have, the more likely we are to obsess over protecting and adding to it. Again, Solomon weighs in with the wisdom of experience: "He who loves money will not be satisfied with money, nor he who loves abundance with its income" (Ecclesiastes 5:10). That's the greedy bent of the human heart—no matter how much you have, it's never enough.

Over the years, I've watched as countless storage facilities have sprung up along the freeways throughout Los Angeles. I've often wondered which possessions people value enough to pay to keep locked away in storage, but which they don't need enough to keep easily accessible? And how many of them are still paying off the credit cards they used to purchase the items that now fill those storage lockers and stalls?

God's people must not succumb to the empty promises of materialism. We need to heed Christ's warning to His disciples about the futility of endless accumulation.

> He said to them, "Beware, and be on your guard against every form of greed; for not even when one has an abundance does his life consist of his possessions." And He told them a parable, saying, "The land of a rich man was very productive. And he began reasoning to himself, saying, 'What shall I do, since I have no place to store my crops?' Then he said, 'This is what I will do: I will tear down my barns and build larger ones, and there I will store all my grain and my goods. And I will say to my soul, "Soul, you have many goods laid up for many years to come; take your ease, eat, drink and be merry."' But God said to him, 'You fool! This very night your soul is required of you; and now who will own what you have prepared?' So is the man who stores up treasure for himself, and is not rich toward God." (Luke 12:15–21)

That's a nightmare scenario for the materialist—to spend his life accumulating a massive fortune only to die before he can spend it. What it illustrates for us is the folly of devoting your life to greedy, materialistic pursuits. We need to see the foolishness and emptiness of such goals before we similarly waste our lives.

The truth is, the things you accumulate and own do not—and cannot—provide you with any security. There are no retirement accounts that are immune to losses, no houses that are impervious to natural disasters. Even if your wealth and possessions do manage to last, *you won't*. You'll never see a hearse pulling a U-Haul trailer. As Paul wrote to Timothy, "We have brought nothing into the world, so we cannot take anything out of it either" (1 Timothy 6:7). Many people have wasted their lives laboring to accumulate more than they could ever hope to spend.

But believing the lies of materialism can lead to more than just a wasted life. Continuing his warning to Timothy, Paul identifies the significant spiritual cost: "Those who want to get rich fall into temptation and a snare and many foolish and harmful desires which plunge men into ruin and destruction. For the love of money is a root of all sorts of evil, and some by longing for it have wandered away from the faith and pierced themselves with many griefs" (vv. 9–10). There's no such thing as a tolerable amount of greed and materialism. God's people need to remember, "No one can serve two masters; for either he will hate the one and love the other, or he will be devoted to one and despise the other. You cannot serve God and wealth" (Matthew 6:24).

To guard against ever-looming temptations of materialism and greed, Christians need to cultivate an attitude of contentment. We need to say with Paul, "If we have food and covering, with these we shall be content" (1 Timothy 6:8). We need to find the most productive, God-honoring uses for those resources with which He blesses us. Ultimately, everything we have in this life is from the Lord. It all belongs to Him; we are merely stewards.

Moreover, we need to understand the truth about the faulty, feeble riches this world has to offer in the first place. Consider the Lord's exhortation in the Sermon on the Mount: "Do not store up for yourselves treasures on earth, where moth and rust destroy, and where thieves break in and steal. But store up for yourselves treasures in heaven, where neither moth nor rust destroys, and where thieves do not break in or steal; for where your treasure is, there your heart will be also" (Matthew 6:19–21). The location of your treasure says a lot about the true nature of your heart. Are you looking to the meager riches of this dead and decaying world for a false sense of stability? Or are your riches in heaven, secure for eternity with your Savior?

We ought to consider one more familiar lie from the world that has contributed to the decline of children born into Christian homes—the illusion of time. Perpetual teens frequently put off responsibilities and tasks that get in the way of what they would rather be doing, counting on time they're not guaranteed. And we know the world is eager to hold off the responsibilities of marriage and family. While they show no compunction about cohabitating, young people are waiting longer than previous generations to get married.[23]

You can see how the procrastination of marriage and family could be linked to the other lies we've previously discussed. Some might be holding off the responsibilities in favor of pursuing their own happiness and fulfillment; others might simply be waiting until they feel more financially secure. In both cases, those motives are undergirded by the false belief that there will be plenty of time later to get married and have children.

But Scripture makes clear that we are not promised the time that many are counting on.

> Come now, you who say, "Today or tomorrow we will go to such and such a city, and spend a year there and engage in business and make a profit." Yet you do not know what your life will be like tomorrow. You are just a vapor that appears for a little while and then vanishes away. Instead, you ought to say, "If the Lord wills, we will live and also do this or that." (James 4:13–15)

The length of our lives is completely out of our control. We can make plans, but our ability to fulfill those plans lies entirely with God. He alone determines whether we wake up each morning, whether our lungs will continue to fill with air and our hearts keep pumping. This fragile life is a blessing that He alone sustains.

Reflecting on the brevity of life, Job said, "My days are swifter than a runner; they flee away.... They slip by like reed boats, like an eagle that swoops on its prey" (Job 9:25–26). He understood that life is fleeting. "Man, who is born of woman, is short-lived and full of turmoil. Like a flower he comes forth and withers. He also flees like a shadow and does not remain" (14:1–2). God's people must not count on time we have not been promised.

It's really a question of humility. Do we live in light of God's sustaining power, or do we assume we have time to spare? It's arrogant and foolish to ignore God's will and His sovereignty over the length of your life. "Do not boast about tomorrow, for you do not know what a day may bring forth" (Proverbs 27:1). The truth is, you might not even see tomorrow. Like the man in Christ's parable in Luke 12, your soul could be required of you this very night.

Does that mean we shouldn't plan ahead? Of course not. The sin of the businessman described in James 4 is not that he planned ahead for his trip. It's that he saw his plans as absolute— he left no room for the will of God. He foolishly assumed the position of sovereignty that belongs to God alone.

Christians need to surrender the illusion of control and the expectation of more time. We can make plans, but they're not where our confidence should reside. Instead, we entrust those plans to God, knowing that He will direct us where He wills. "Trust in the LORD with all your heart and do not lean on your own understanding. In all your ways acknowledge Him, and He will make your paths straight" (Proverbs 3:5–6).

And although it might sound strange, routinely reflecting on the brevity and fragility of life is a good habit for believers. While such contemplation would be depressing and frightening for unrepentant sinners who have no hope beyond this world, God's people need not fear death and the grave. With the hope of heaven, we can eagerly look beyond this fleeting life to our eternal home. That perspective ought to purge our hearts of any love for this world and its distractions, bringing focus and purpose to the life the Lord continues to grant us. As Moses wrote in Psalm 90, reflecting on the brevity of life would "teach us to number our days, that we may present to [God] a heart of wisdom" (v. 12). If nothing else, it would keep us from wasting time that is meant for the work of the kingdom and the growth of godly homes.

We could endlessly speculate on other factors that might be contributing to the hesitancy of young Christians when it comes to marriage and children. But the more pressing question is: How do we best encourage those young men and women in the church who are holding back from starting families?

In short, we need to remind them that they are missing out on God's primary blessings in this life.

Remember that the apostle Peter refers to marriage as "the grace of life" (1 Peter 3:7), and in Ephesians 5, Paul describes marriage as a picture of God's relationship to His church. It's a God-ordained union in which two people are unbreakably bonded together, united in mind, will, spirit, body, and emotion. It's not an arm's-length relationship. In marriage two people become one flesh, sacrificed to one another before the Lord. It's a mutual covenant in which each spouse becomes the exclusive, consecrated possession of the other person.

Moreover, marriage is God's work. Describing the unique bond of marriage, Jesus said, "So they are no longer two, but one flesh. What therefore God has joined together, let no man separate" (Matthew 19:6). Marriages aren't casual relationships, and they don't happen by coincidence. Each one has been foreordained by God for His eternal purposes.

Consider how prominently marriage figures in the work of creation. God breathes life into Adam and places him in the garden, then immediately declares, "It is not good for the man to be alone; I will make him a helper suitable for him" (Genesis 2:18). Scripture tells us that no suitable helper was found among God's creation, so He crafted one specifically for Adam.

> So the LORD God caused a deep sleep to fall upon the man, and he slept; then He took one of his ribs and closed up the flesh at that place. The LORD God fashioned into a woman the rib which He had taken from the man, and brought her to the man. The man said, "This is now bone of my bones, and flesh of my flesh; she shall be called Woman, because she was taken out of Man." For this reason a man shall leave his father and his mother, and be joined to his wife; and they shall become one flesh. (vv. 21–24)

It's not good for us to be alone. That wasn't God's design from the beginning. True, some people have been called to singleness and equipped for celibacy—often in relation to their unique service to the Lord and His church. But the vast majority of people still have those God-given desires for intimacy that are meant to be fulfilled only in marriage.

And in God's good design, that's how He brings about the other primary blessing of this life: children. As we have noted repeatedly in this book, Scripture declares emphatically that children are blessings from God. These are all key texts, and well worth revisiting. In Deuteronomy 7:12–13, God promises Israel,

> Then it shall come about, because you listen to these judgments and keep and do them, that the LORD your God will keep with you His covenant and His lovingkindness which He swore to your forefathers. He will love you and bless you and multiply you; He will also bless the fruit of your womb and the fruit of your ground.

Psalm 113 extols the greatness of the Lord and His mercy and grace to the poor and needy. As we noted much earlier in this book, that psalm concludes with these words extolling the virtue and the joy of motherhood: "He makes the barren woman abide in the house as a joyful mother of children. Praise the LORD!" (v. 9).

Psalm 127:3–5 is that familiar text where Solomon makes the point as explicit as possible: "Behold, children are a gift of the LORD, the fruit of the womb is a reward. Like arrows in the hand of a warrior, so are the children of one's youth. How blessed is the man whose quiver is full of them; they will not be ashamed when they speak with their enemies in the gate." And as we have already seen, Psalm 128 continues and expands on that same theme.

Children are not an intrusion; they're a blessing from the Lord. Consider how God repeatedly displayed His grace and mercy by opening the wombs of His chosen servants. He gave Sarah a son long after her childbearing days were supposedly past (Genesis 18:11–14). He took pity on Leah because she was unloved, opening her womb and giving her and Jacob four sons (29:31–35). Every conception, every child is a creation of God.

After Boaz married Ruth, "the LORD enabled her to conceive, and she gave birth to a son" (Ruth 4:13). Scripture records how the women congratulated her mother-in-law Naomi, who had previously lost her husband and sons. "Blessed is the LORD who has not left you without a redeemer today.... May he also be to you a restorer of life and a sustainer of your old age" (vv. 14–15). That idea is becoming increasingly important to me, as I have children who will soon need to take care of me. What a blessing they are—it's truly incomprehensible. There are no words to describe how much I love my children and grandchildren and great-grandchildren. They are my life.

We who have been so richly blessed with children by God need to live out the joys of parenthood for younger men and women in the church. They need to behold God's goodness to us. No family is perfect, and the struggles of parenting are plentiful and obvious. But those around us need to see and hear firsthand from us the immense, divine blessing that our families are, if they're going to aspire to similar blessings themselves.

# CHAPTER SEVEN

# THE ATTACK ON LIFE

The safest place for a child ought to be his mother's womb. It's where the child is at his most vulnerable state, and it's where he should be most lovingly nurtured and protected. However, thanks to the epidemic of abortion, the womb has become the most deadly battlefield in the war on children. Unborn children are being massacred in staggering numbers.

*Massacre* is exactly the right word. The world's efforts to snuff out the lives of unborn children is by magnitudes the worst pogrom in a century that has been marred by more appalling genocides, mass killings, and ethnic cleansings than any other time in human history. In America alone, it is estimated that more than 62.5 million children have been slaughtered in the womb since abortion was legalized in 1973.[24] To put that number into perspective, it's more than the combined populations of Florida, New York, and Pennsylvania (our third, fourth, and fifth most populated states).[25] It's more than double the population of Texas (which ranks second). You could wipe out the entire west coast of the United States—California (first), Oregon (twenty-seventh), and Washington (thirteenth)—and still be more than ten million short of the number of babies America has legally murdered in the womb.

That's an appalling number, and it should leave us stunned and horrified. But it pales in comparison to global totals.

The World Health Organization estimates "around 73 million induced abortions take place worldwide each year."[26] You read that correctly—*73 million each year*! That would be like wiping out the entire populations of California, Texas, and Oregon, *year after year*. It means the slaughter never stops, as the world is perpetually murdering more than two babies every second, around the clock, for a full calendar year. That monstrous global holocaust has become an annual routine.

How did we get here? It wasn't that long ago that abortion proponents were lobbying for the practice to be "safe, legal, and rare." That phrase—coined by Bill Clinton in 1992, while he was running for president—provided some reassurance to pro-choicers who were still uncomfortable with the grotesqueries of killing children in the womb.

But thirty years later, that notion of "rare" abortions has been completely dismissed. Tulsi Gabbard was pilloried for using that phrase verbatim to clarify her position on abortion in a debate during the 2019 presidential primary. Gabbard was actually quoting both Clintons. Hillary Clinton had borrowed and expanded on her husband's line during her failed 2008 presidential campaign, saying, "I believe abortion should be safe, legal, and rare, and when I say, 'rare,' I mean *rare*."[27] Realizing that sentiment no longer played well with liberal feminist audiences, the Democratic Party dropped the word "rare" from its platform altogether in 2012, and Mrs. Clinton did the same during her second failed campaign in 2016.[28]

But the reaction to Gabbard's statement illustrates with unmistakable clarity how the fanaticism over abortion has grown in recent decades. Nothing less than a full-throated, cheerleading-style endorsement will be tolerated. One author accused Gabbard of resorting "to a controversial decades-old talking point that pro-choice supporters say only further stigmatizes abortion at a critical moment."[29] Because heaven forbid we *stigmatize* the murder of babies in the womb.

Abortion proponents want to deny that there is anything unpleasant about abortion; they want it to be viewed as just another medical procedure. They relentlessly refer to it as "healthcare." That redefinition is supposed to eliminate any discussion of rarity or regret, or any concessions about the immorality of the abortion industry. Here's how another abortion activist reacted to Gabbard's words: "I cannot think of a less compelling way to advocate for something than saying that it should be rare." She continued, "Anyone who uses that phrase is operating from the assumption that abortion is a bad thing."[30]

That quote comes from Amelia Bonow, the cofounder of the website Shout Your Abortion, which encourages women to share the stories of their abortions to normalize and destigmatize the practice. The titles alone give you an indication of the ghoulish content to be found there: "Never Sorry About My Abortion," "My Abortion Made Me Happy," "Third Pregnancy, Second Abortion, and I Am Not Ashamed," "The Only Thing I Ever Felt About the Abortion Was Relief," "I Don't Feel Guilty in the Slightest," and "My Abortions Made Me a Better Mother." The wickedness of the unregenerate heart says that the murder of a child is both empowering and praiseworthy.

Meanwhile, politicians continue to look for ways to make it easier than ever to murder unwanted children in the womb.

In January 2019, the New York state legislature enacted the Reproductive Health Act, which both expanded access to abortions and relaxed restrictions on who could provide them, while removing some of the criminal penalties related to the death of an unborn child. Specifically, it legalized abortion when "the patient is within twenty-four weeks from the commencement of pregnancy, or there is an absence of fetal viability, or *the abortion is necessary to protect the patient's life or health*" (emphasis added).[31] The law doesn't specify *how* a mother's health must be in danger— it leaves broad room for interpretation as to what constitutes a detriment to her health, and gives the ultimate decision-making authority to the one providing the abortion. However, the law is carefully worded to define away the personhood of the unborn: "'Person,' when referring to the victim of a homicide, means a human being who has been born and is alive."[32]

Critics rightly interpreted the law as effectively legalizing infanticide. Prior to the Reproductive Health Act, New York did not permit an abortion after twenty-four weeks, except in cases where the mother's life was threatened.[33] But by expanding that to any threat to her *health*, by carefully avoiding any clear definition of what that means, and by refusing to differentiate between physical and mental health—they've thrown wide the doors for endless subjective interpretation and almost certain abuse. If a woman were to decide, while on the verge of giving birth, that her child somehow represented a threat to her mental health, a willing doctor (or a nurse practitioner, physician's assistant, or midwife, under New York's expanded regulations) has the authority to provide the abortion. It means that legally murdering the child in your womb is as simple as thinking up an excuse. In only the most twisted minds would that qualify as "reproductive health."

Around the same time, the Virginia State Legislature was considering a similar bill that would have likewise broadened state regulations on late-term abortions. The bill, known as The Repeal Act (HB 2491), was set to remove aspects of existing Virginia state laws that restricted abortions. The bill's author, Democratic delegate Kathy Tran, acknowledged that it would permit abortions late into the third trimester, even up until birth. When pressed to answer whether a dilating woman could request an abortion if a doctor would certify that the birth could impair the mental health of the woman, Tran said, "My bill would allow that, yes."[34]

In the uproar that followed, Virginia's then-governor Ralph Northam—a former Army doctor and pediatric neurologist—expressed his opinion about the bill as well. He defended his Democratic colleague and the supposed aims of the controversial legislation. But the hypothetical scenario he painted only further raised concerns about how the bill would legalize infanticide. He said, "In this particular example, if a mother is in labor, I can tell you exactly what would happen: The infant would be delivered, the infant would be kept comfortable, the infant would be resuscitated if that's what the mother and the family desired, and then a discussion would ensue between the physicians and the mother."[35] Northam's explanation rightly horrified listeners across the country, as he seemed to acknowledge that newborns could be denied care while their mothers wrestled with buyer's remorse—that a baby that had been successfully delivered might still be threatened by abortion. Mercifully, the bill was struck down and failed to become Virginia state law.

In the aftermath of the controversy, Nebraska Senator Ben Sasse reintroduced his Born-Alive Abortion Survivors Protection Act, designed to secure nationwide protections for babies that

survive attempted abortions. The bill once again failed to pass—
and it has failed with each subsequent attempt.

Prompted by the failure of the federal government, some
states have taken steps to individually limit access to abortion.
Alabama, Kentucky, South Dakota, and Wyoming all instituted
laws protecting children born after attempted abortions. Others
like Idaho, Oklahoma, and South Carolina outlawed abortion after
a fetal heartbeat has been detected (with some exceptions in the
case of medical emergencies or life-threatening circumstances
for the mother).[36] Texas likewise enacted a heartbeat bill that
prohibits abortions as early as six weeks into the pregnancy.

The one somewhat encouraging development in more than
fifty years of unbridled abortion-industry growth finally came on
June 24, 2022, when the United States Supreme Court ruled in the
case of Dobbs v. Jackson Women's Health Organization that the
constitution does not guarantee women any inalienable right to
have an abortion. This ruling effectively nullified Roe v. Wade as
well as the Court's 1992 decision in Planned Parenthood v. Casey.
It freed the states to enact their own laws restricting abortion
and thus virtually guaranteed that some states would end their
participation in the slaughter.

Nevertheless (and contrary to much of the angry rhetoric
from pro-abortion lobbyists), the Court's decision does not
*automatically* restrict abortion. It has, however, mobilized pro-
abortion protestors and liberal legislators to propose new, more
liberal laws that would make late-term abortions easier to obtain
in states and cities run by pro-abortion officials. The decision
was certainly a rare victory for pro-life advocates, but it is by no
means a final triumph over those waging war against the very
lives of children.

Several states already had protections written into their laws in case the Supreme Court overturned Roe v. Wade. For example, in December 2021, months before the Supreme Court decision was issued, California Governor Gavin Newsom unveiled his plan to make his state a "sanctuary" for those seeking abortions. His proposal is for the state to cover travel, housing, and medical expenses for anyone intent on murdering their child in the womb.[37]

Why are so many politicians intent on keeping abortion available? What prompts this insatiable bloodlust? In a word, *money*.

Planned Parenthood is the nation's largest abortion provider. With more than six hundred centers across the country,[38] they murder hundreds of thousands of children in the womb every year. Between October 1, 2018 and September 30, 2019, they performed 354,871 abortion procedures,[39] more than half the total number reported to the CDC in 2019.[40] For their work, they received over $618 million from government health service reimbursements and grants.[41]

But not all that money goes toward murdering babies in the womb. A significant portion of their funding is invested back into politicians who will support and expand abortion rights. It turns out that Planned Parenthood wields significant political influence in local, state, and federal elections. In the 2020 election cycle alone, they spent $45 million[42] to promote and support candidates who defend abortion in order to keep their evil but lucrative industry legal.

The obscene profiteering within this industry includes significant money that is made from harvesting and selling the fetal tissue of babies killed in the womb.

In 2015, pro-life activist David Daleiden and the Center for Medical Progress released an undercover video proving that Planned Parenthood was selling body parts from aborted and dismembered babies. Though federal law states that "it shall be unlawful for any person to knowingly acquire, receive, or otherwise transfer any human fetal tissue for valuable consideration," authorities filed no charges against Planned Parenthood.[43] They indicted Daleiden on multiple counts, accusing him of fraud, conspiracy, and unlawful recording of conversations.

The videos clearly showed Planned Parenthood employees and other abortion providers negotiating prices for the sale of fetal specimens. People who did not realize they were being recorded described the ghastly means through which fetal body parts were procured. The recordings featured abortion doctors detailing the procedures by which they are able to keep an aborted child's body intact for body parts.[44] Others explained methods they use designed to tear the aborted baby's body apart purposely to insure that it would not resemble a baby upon removal.[45]

The hidden-camera videos exposed these so-called "healthcare workers" haggling over the value of aborted fetal tissue—hearts, brains, livers, kidneys, and thymus glands, in particular—and how they expected to be compensated for the extra work required to secure the organs. One callously jokes that she wanted a Lamborghini.[46] That's how flippantly these ghoulish butchers view the lives of precious children—and how little they even try to disguise their disdain for God's creation.

As we discussed in chapter 2, abortion is the twenty-first century equivalent of Molech worship, and those who champion the practice actually treat it as something akin to a religious sacrament. But it is in reality the grossest kind of sin directly against God, because children from the moment of conception belong uniquely to Him. Bear in mind that God speaks of infants and toddlers as "My children," and Jesus welcomed infants into His arms and said, "The kingdom of heaven belongs to such as these" (Matthew 19:14). That was the whole point we stressed in chapter 2—namely that children do not belong to the government, or to society in general, or even to their parents. In a special way, little ones too young to make their own moral decisions belong uniquely to God. He has placed them in the care of their parents, and the parents' role is one of stewardship, not ownership.

That reality must surely frame our view of abortion. Every tiny life conceived is a creation of God, belonging to Him, and deserving protection and nurturing for His glory. From their inception as zygotes, every child is an immortal person, made by God in His image. And the Lord promises to judge fiercely those who shed the blood of His children. Here again is Ezekiel 16:36–38:

> Thus says the Lord GOD, "Because your lewdness was poured out and your nakedness uncovered through your harlotries with your lovers and with all your detestable idols, and *because of the blood of your sons which you gave to idols*, therefore, behold, I will gather all your lovers with whom you took pleasure, even all those whom you loved and all those whom you hated. So I will gather them against you from every direction and expose your nakedness to them that they may see all your nakedness. Thus I will judge you like women who commit adultery or shed blood are judged; and I will bring on you the blood of wrath and jealousy."

Notice: the underlying evil that motivates people to slaughter helpless children is spiritual adultery. Here is perhaps the most vivid proof of how thoroughly evil false religion (including postmodern agnosticism) really is.

As we noted in an earlier chapter, God's condemnation of those who participated in this deadly spiritual adultery was harsh and unstinted. He totally closed His ears to their prayers and refused to receive their worship (Ezekiel 20:30–31). The message was clear: Don't expect God to honor your show of devotion to Him if you're also worshiping these false, pagan gods. Don't come looking to Him for blessing and favor if you're also trying to earn approbation from idols through lewd worship and child sacrifice.

We've seen already how rather than avoiding the pagan practices of the surrounding nations, Israel dove headlong into their corruption. They defiled themselves and the worship of the one, true God with their participation in such wickedness.

We rightly recoil at the thought of ancient child sacrifice. Why is it so difficult for people in our culture to see that the abortion industry is perpetrating the very same evil—and doing it on a vastly larger scale? The only difference is in the gods: Ancient pagans were trying to appease crude carvings of wood, stone, and metal. Those have been replaced with the idol of self, which is arguably even more evil.

One of the most common refrains from those trying to justify the carnage of abortion is, "If I hadn't had an abortion, I couldn't have—." Lots of different things (all self-serving, temporal, or materialistic idols) complete that sentence: career goals, awards and accolades, and all manner of personal achievements. These would presumably have been hindered by an inconvenient pregnancy. And perhaps those things would have been impossible for someone with a child to care for. (In most cases, we'll never know.) But consider how evil any flavor of consuming, corrupting self-love must be in order to trade a precious little life for the sake of personal priorities and achievements.

And how is that supposed to be any different from hurling babies into the flames in the hopes of obtaining a plentiful crop, much-needed rain, or good fortune from the gods? The worship of Molech is still alive today, and thriving.

The abortion lobby has dominated our culture for decades. They have convinced a large bloc of legislators and much of our court system that abortion is an unassailable right and a practical necessity. Christians need to see the world differently. Specifically, we need to cultivate heaven's perspective on human life. We must understand what Scripture teaches when it comes to the genocide of abortion.

To begin with, we need to get rid of the notion that any child is an accident. True, the pregnancy might not have been planned by the parents, but that's not to say that it happened outside of anyone's control. In God's sovereignty, there are no accidents—every conception is an act of His creative work.

We've already considered several instances where the Old Testament tells us that God alone opens and closes the womb according to His will. The apostle Paul made a similar point in his confrontation with the philosophers in Athens. In the Areopagus on Mars Hill, surrounded by the multitude of false gods that dominated all aspects of ancient life, Paul attempted to introduce these pagans to the one, true God.

> Men of Athens, I observe that you are very religious in all respects. For while I was passing through and examining the objects of your worship, I also found an altar with this inscription, "TO AN UNKNOWN GOD." Therefore what you worship in ignorance, this I proclaim to you. The God who made the world and all things in it, since He is Lord of heaven and earth, does not dwell in temples made with hands; nor is He served by human hands, as though He needed anything, since He Himself gives to all people life and breath and all things. (Acts 17:22–25)

Unlike the dull and dumb idols that surrounded them, the God of the Bible doesn't need anything from people—the Creator of everything doesn't require the assistance of humans. Rather, Paul says, *He made us.* In the words of John's gospel, "All things came into being through Him, and apart from Him nothing came into being that has come into being" (John 1:3).

Paul continued to extol the Lord's creative work, saying, "He made from one man every nation of mankind to live on all the face of the earth, having determined their appointed times and the boundaries of their habitation" (Acts 17:26). We think of the intimate work God did in creating Adam, but throughout Adam's line God's creative work has continued. You and I were just as expertly formed by our Creator. And His work didn't end there—our Creator is also our Sustainer. Paul says, "For in Him we live and move and exist" (v. 28). We are not the handiwork of some distant deity. God is personally and intimately involved in creating and sustaining every life.

Psalm 139 is that familiar psalm of David that illustrates and extols God's omniscience, omnipresence, and His role in the creation of each individual. David, speaking directly to God, says, "You formed my inward parts" (v. 13). The Hebrew word he uses literally describes the kidneys, but the term referred to the entire complex of organs that make up the human anatomy. We're not just a clump of cells and tissue that developed by accident—God Himself oversees the formation of all our internal organs.

This psalm, though familiar, deserves the most careful attention. Verse 13 continues, "You wove me in my mother's womb." We know more today about biology, chemistry, and chromosomes than David possibly could have, but the language he used under the inspiration of the Holy Spirit is nonetheless precise. It is God alone who weaves together the strands of DNA that form our unique genetic code. David was rightly in awe of this divine work: "I will give thanks to You, for I am fearfully and wonderfully made; wonderful are Your works, and my soul knows it very well" (v. 14). We should be equally staggered that the God of the universe was so intimately involved in designing and crafting us at conception.

David writes, "My frame was not hidden from You, when I was made in secret, and skillfully wrought in the depths of the earth" (v. 15). "Frame" refers to his structure—the bones, muscles, ligaments, and tendons that form and support his body. "The depths of the earth" serves as a euphemism for the womb, meaning that it is God alone who performs this technical, structural work in secret, out of the sight or influence of anyone else.

The description of this intimate, creative work concludes with the statement, "Your eyes have seen my unformed substance" (v. 16). God alone knows in the most minute detail exactly what you and I looked like as embryos. He is the only one who has truly known us from the start, controlling and overseeing every aspect of our gestation all the way up to our birth. Long before our mothers and fathers laid eyes on us, God knew what we looked like. More than that—He determined what we would look like.

But God's authority and oversight go well beyond His work in the womb. David continues, "In Your book were all written the days that were ordained *for me,* when as yet there was not one of them" (v. 16). God knows intimately everything about you from the time of your conception because He made you, just as He made every person who has been conceived. You're not a biological accident. You're a creation of God. You belong to Him.

Flowing out of God's creative work in every person comes another key feature of heaven's view of human life: We are all created in the image of God. In Genesis 1:26, "God said, 'Let Us make man in Our image, according to Our likeness.'" Verse 27 confirms, "God created man in His own image." That doesn't mean we look like God—that we share physical similarities. Rather, it's a statement about our moral and spiritual capacity.

Some aspects of God's nature and character are exclusive to Him; theologians refer to them as His *incommunicable* attributes. God alone is omnipotent, omniscient, and omnipresent. Although we were made in His image, no man is all powerful, all knowing, or present everywhere at once. And while we are immortal and will exist forever, we are not eternal—only God existed in eternity past. Immutability is another attribute that belongs to God alone. Only He is truly changeless and perfectly consistent.

But humans have the capacity to display other attributes that mirror the character of God in ways no other created animal can. Of all God's creatures, we are uniquely made in His image. Many of these qualities have to do with personhood and our ability to have relationships—those things that make human life *human*. We can love meaningfully and hate for righteous reasons. We can think, and reflect, and feel, and understand. We have consciences and moral sensibilities, so we understand the fundamental concepts of good and evil. We can make rational choices and act on them deliberately. All of those features of humanity are given to us as part of the image of God.

And Scripture demands that we respect that aspect of God's design in each other. Describing the hypocrisy of an untamed tongue, James 3:9 says, "With it we bless our Lord and Father, and with it we curse men, who have been made in the likeness of God." No matter who the other person is—and no matter how he or she might have wronged us—we need to recognize that they were made in the image of God, and treat them accordingly.

Scripture even identifies the image of God as the basis for capital punishment. Genesis 9:6 says, "Whoever sheds man's blood, by man his blood shall be shed, for in the image of God He made man." Killing someone made in the image of God means you forfeit your own life. Christ upheld that principle in the New Testament. When the Romans came to arrest Jesus, Peter grabbed a sword and began to fight, lopping off the ear of the High Priest's slave. Rebuking Peter, Jesus said, "Put your sword back into its place; for all those who take up the sword shall perish by the sword" (Matthew 26:52). If you take a life, yours can be taken as punishment.

We need to remember the sacredness of human life, especially as it pertains to abortion. That unborn baby is not merely a mass of cells and tissue that can be carelessly discarded. That little life is not merely a part of the mother's body until she decides to have it removed. Abortion means killing another person who was created by God to bear His image.

God's Word repeatedly commands His people to care for the weak and defenseless. Psalm 82 says, "Vindicate the weak and fatherless; do justice to the afflicted and destitute. Rescue the weak and needy; deliver them out of the hand of the wicked" (vv. 3–4). James identifies "visit[ing] orphans and widows in their distress" as a key feature of "pure and undefiled religion" (James 1:27).

God's loving care extends to the most weak and defenseless— an unborn child—in that He has placed that precious life in the place of ultimate protection, provision, and safety: the womb of its mother. Moreover, He has built into each mother a natural instinct to love and protect her children. In His design, the mother's womb is a sanctuary of protection for that helpless, unborn infant to enjoy. What an inconceivable and heinous crime it is to invade that special sanctum of rest, peace, and nourishment, violate the unique protection it provides, and purposely dismember the tiny human whose place of security and safekeeping that was supposed to be.

The Lord even built into His law specific protections for the unborn. In Exodus 21, He outlines the following scenario: "If men struggle with each other and strike a woman with child so that she gives birth prematurely, yet there is no injury, he shall surely be fined as the woman's husband may demand of him, and he shall pay as the judges decide. But if there is any further injury, then you shall appoint as a penalty life for life, eye for eye, tooth for tooth, hand for hand, foot for foot, burn for burn, wound for wound, bruise for bruise" (vv. 22–25). This is *lex talionis*, the law of retribution that demands like-for-like punishment. That law defined how the Israelites were to punish crimes between people that resulted in personal injury and death. Here the Lord extends those same protections to unborn children.

It's also worth noting that Scripture uses the same Hebrew word, *yeled*, to describe children both in and out of the womb (cf. Luke 1:41, 44 and 2:12, 16). In heaven's view, there is no distinction.

From God's perspective, killing an unborn child in his mother's womb is the same as killing any other person. In the care and compassion of His good design, those who are the most weak, helpless, and defenseless are also the most protected. It's nothing short of a Satanic assault to invade the sanctity of the womb and rip that little life to shreds in what was designed to be the place of greatest safety and protection.

God condemns every kind of murder in no uncertain terms. His law is explicit: "You shall not murder" (Exodus 20:13). Scripture tells us the Lord hates "hands that shed innocent blood" (Proverbs 6:17). He will not permit murderers to go unpunished.

When Cain killed Abel, God confronted him with these stunning words: "What have you done? The voice of your brother's blood is crying to Me from the ground" (Genesis 4:10). Throughout the Old Testament, the blood of those slaughtered cries out to God for justice. So also David exclaims in 2 Samuel 4:11: "How much more, when wicked men have killed a righteous man in his own house on his bed, shall I not now require his blood from your hand and destroy you from the earth?" Blood requires blood. That is the law of God.

Nothing illustrates more starkly the moral collapse of a society than the mass murder of little ones in the wombs of their mothers. We are no better than those ancient nations that slaughtered the innocent by feeding their children to idols as fuel for the flames of their pagan altars. And we are headed for the same swift judgment. This land is soaked in the blood of millions and millions of babies murdered in the womb, and it's crying out for justice. That is the truth about abortion that we need to bring to a world awash in the blood of murdered babies.

In the same breath, we need to tell the world that there is still hope for those who have murdered their children. They can find complete forgiveness and restoration in Christ. Paul did; he confessed, "I was formerly a blasphemer and a persecutor and a violent aggressor. Yet I was shown mercy" (1 Timothy 1:13). God's grace is sufficient for the victims of abortion. It is sufficient for their murderers, too.

# CHAPTER EIGHT

# THE ATTACK ON THE FAMILY

We think a lot about terrorist attacks in America. Virtually anyone you talk to can give you a rundown of the most destructive acts of terror that have been perpetrated against this country.

But let me suggest to you that the greatest terror attacks against the United States didn't come from any foreign entity or homegrown enemy. They weren't the work of Islamic fascists, social anarchists, or white supremacists. Rather, the two greatest acts of terror against America have been perpetrated by the United States Supreme Court.

The first, as we have just discussed, was the legalization of abortion, leading to tens of millions of babies slaughtered in the womb. It's a staggering death toll, and an incalculable cost to our country. The blood of those precious lives cries out from the ground for divine vengeance on this nation.

The second great act of terror by the Supreme Court was the legalization of same-sex marriage. On June 26, 2015, the nation's highest court ruled 5–4 in the case of Obergefell v. Hodges, requiring all US states and territories to perform same-sex marriages and recognize them as equal in rights and privileges to opposite-sex unions.

Make no mistake, these are deeply consequential decisions—direct assaults on the well-being of humanity. With the legalization of abortion, the Supreme Court gave people the ability to destroy life in the womb. It was effectively the destruction of motherhood. And through the radical redefinition of marriage, they have effectively destroyed the family. There's no explosion, virus, toxin, or weapon of mass destruction that comes anywhere near to that kind of devastation. Through this all-out attack on the family, our country is being terrorized by those who are most responsible to protect it.

No human court has the authority to redefine morality. But the Supreme Court has said murder is not murder, and marriage is not marriage. They've effectively said a family is whatever anyone wants it to be. In attempting to redefine these fundamental aspects of life, they have usurped authority that belongs exclusively to God, who is the Creator of life, marriage, and family.

All such attempts to redefine morality apart from God's Word and His design are acts of rebellion and blasphemy against our Creator, His holy nature, and His divine authority. The Supreme Court of the United States has taken a deliberate position against God. Most of Western society, starting at the highest levels of government, agrees with the Supreme Court. Such blasphemous rebellion is energized by the accumulated corruption of sinful human hearts. But behind that collection of sinful hearts is the realm of satanic forces. Scripture tells us Satan holds this world under his sinister, oppressive command: "The whole world lies in the power of the evil one" (1 John 5:19). Satan rules this world of sinners, and he has his power in high places. He oversees this kingdom of darkness. He's the enemy of the triune God, His

Word, and His church, and he seeks to destroy all that is good, pure, virtuous, and true.

That is to say, we don't need to be surprised when evil surrounds and encroaches on us. For a brief window of a few hundred years, the Western world—and America, in particular— enjoyed something of a reprieve from the normal level of spiritual conflict and the relentless persecution that have plagued God's people since Adam's fall. The prevailing influence of Christian morality granted us this relatively brief respite, but it has come to a screeching halt.

In other words, the rebellion and blasphemy we're seeing run rampant in society today is not an anomaly. The anomaly was the fleeting period when the Western world was willing to follow along with general Christian ethics and morality. The moral decay and descent into satanic rebellion we're seeing today is just this wicked world reverting to its usual pattern. In Jesus' words, "If the world hates you, you know that it has hated Me before it hated you. If you were of the world, the world would love its own; but because you are not of the world, but I chose you out of the world, because of this the world hates you.... 'A slave is not greater than his master.' If they persecuted Me, they will also persecute you; if they kept My word, they will keep yours also" (John 15:18–20).

As society grows more inhospitable to God's people and His truth, we need to recognize where the true battleground lies. The world isn't merely interested in redefining marriage. Their goals are far more destructive. As one homosexual author and activist put it,

> It's a no-brainer that [homosexuals] should have the right to marry, but I also think equally that it's a no-brainer that the

institution of marriage should not exist.... Fighting for gay
marriage generally involves lying about what we are going to
do with marriage when we get there—because we lie that the
institution of marriage is not going to change, and that is a lie.

The institution of marriage is going to change, and it should
change. And again, I don't think it should exist.[47]

So, their aim isn't simply to rethink gender roles and
what defines a family. This controversy is not *really* about
recognizing civil rights and celebrating homosexual marriage,
transgenderism, or any of the other sexual perversions du jour.
The world's primary objective is to destroy what God has designed.

The family unit is vital to God's design for an ordered,
sensible civilization. It's a key feature of His common grace to all
humanity. He designed the family as the means to pass on truth,
order, peace, and temporal blessing from one generation to the
next. That's why the family as God designed it is perpetually in
Satan's crosshairs.

Families provide a sovereign unit that acts as a barrier
against the corruption that dominates this world. When you
shatter the family, that small barrier disintegrates. It removes all
the guardrails God put in place to help raise and shape children
into adults. It means you no longer have privacy or authority in
your own home. In fact, it hijacks children altogether. Without
the family unit, they no longer belong to you but to the public,
ensnared by an evil education system and bound to the whims of
godless politicians and wicked ideologues and leaders. Without
the protection of the family, children are turned over to influences
that encourage them to question all forms of authority and even
doubt the obvious facts of their own identity.

Consider how few protections are in place for children when the family falls apart. They're turned over to teachers, many of whom want to poison their minds with liberal and socialist ideologies. They become enthralled with entertainers who corrupt and hypersexualize them before they ever reach puberty. They are given into the care of depraved behavioral specialists and medical quacks who have an agenda to help them defy biological realities by mutilating their bodies. And they are exploited by politicians who want to make them totally dependent on the government to fulfill all their needs. Destroying the family is crucial to Satan's battle plan in the war on children.

The goal of feminism was never merely equal rights in marriage. Satan's aim is the total obliteration of the family. He wants no private, ordered households that can withstand his corrupting influence. He will stand no loving defense or spiritual nurturing for young, impressionable minds. He opposes biblical morality. The devil wants children immersed in the wickedness of the world as early as possible.

The attack on the family is not a new strategy for the powers of evil, and it didn't begin with the legalization of same-sex marriage. The destruction of God's design for the family has been one of Satan's primary goals from the beginning. God made His intentions for marriage and family clear from the outset. Remember that in the beginning, "God created man in His own image, in the image of God He created him; male and female He created them. God blessed them; and God said to them, 'Be fruitful and multiply, and fill the earth'" (Genesis 1:27–28). At the very dawn of creation, the Lord declared His plan for the human race. He brought a man and a woman together—two people, different genders, in union for life—so that they could bring forth children. But you don't get very far into the book of Genesis before you run into Satan's perversions of God's design: adultery, fornication, polygamy, incest, prostitution, and homosexuality. Such corruptions have dominated human society, starting in the very first generation after the Fall.

By the time of Christ, divorce was a serious threat to the sanctity of the family. In first-century Israel, the dissolution of a marriage was merely a matter of paperwork. A man could divorce his wife for a variety of reasons.[48]

Therefore, in His Sermon on the Mount, Jesus exposed the hypocrisy and legalism that dominated Jewish faith and practice. Marriage was one of the themes our Lord specifically stressed. He said, "It was said, 'Whoever sends his wife away, let him give her a certificate of divorce'; but I say to you that everyone who divorces his wife, except for the reason of unchastity, makes her commit adultery; and whoever marries a divorced woman commits adultery" (Matthew 5:31–32).

The predominance of divorce stemmed from a popular rabbinical interpretation of Deuteronomy 24:1, which, in the original context of God's law, sets up a scenario dealing with divorce and remarriage. The verse says, "When a man takes a wife and marries her, and it happens that she finds no favor in his eyes because he has found some indecency in her, and he writes her a certificate of divorce and puts it in her hand and sends her out from his house…" The truth is, that verse alone doesn't even complete the thought intended by God—the point of the passage was not to make divorce a simple matter. It simply acknowledged that divorce was inevitable in marriages between two sinners, and therefore the law established some restrictive parameters for remarriage. It was supposed to be a disincentive for divorce. Nevertheless, Deuteronomy 24:1 was used as if it gave free permission to men who simply wanted to abandon their wives and families.

Rabbinical tradition significantly broadened the concept of what it meant for a wife to find "no favor in [her husband's] eyes because he has found some indecency in her"—falsely legitimizing all sorts of petty reasons for divorce. The rabbis taught, for example, that a Jewish man could divorce his wife if she spoiled his dinner. He could legally obtain a divorce if his supper was too salty. A man could also divorce his wife if she walked around in public with her head uncovered, or if she talked to other men in the streets. He could abandon his marriage if his wife argued with him or said anything disparaging about his mother. Some even taught that a man could leave his wife simply because he found somebody prettier, who found *more* favor in his eyes.[49]

This overt abuse of Scripture and perversion of God's design gave men license to abandon their wives at will. Women were therefore abandoned by their husbands and left with virtually nothing. As long as the certificate of divorce was filled out correctly, any marriage could be dissolved at any time, for almost any conceivable reason.

The family unit wasn't any more stable or secure in the secular world. Gentiles, of course, did not have to worry about Old Testament technicalities. A man who had the status of citizenship in the Roman world did not have to offer *any* justification for what he did to his wife. He could simply live in blatant disregard for marital fidelity if he wanted. Multitudes of men did precisely that.

Pagan religious practices offered people all the opportunities they could want to indulge their fleshly desires. Communing with the gods frequently included drunken orgies with temple priestesses, who functioned as sacred prostitutes. Harlotry and sexual immorality were peddled under a religious veneer, and that kind of paganism dominated the Gentile world. Home and family life were all but extinct. The famous Greek orator Demosthenes said, "Mistresses we keep for the sake of pleasure, concubines for the daily care of our persons, but wives to bear us legitimate children and to be faithful guardians of our households."[50] The Gentile wife was there to keep house and make babies; nothing more.

In most ancient societies, there wasn't a specific legal procedure for divorce. If a man wanted out of a marriage, he simply put his wife out of his home. However, there wasn't much need for divorce when marital fidelity was not expected or even encouraged. Societies in the pagan world were designed to fulfill every imaginable immoral appetite—fornication, homosexuality, pedophilia, bestiality, and all other unspeakable forms of lust dominated virtually every aspect of daily life.

We rightly recoil at the thought of such pervasive perversions. But the twenty-first century world isn't doing any better when it comes to defending morality and adhering to God's design for the family. In fact, modern society has succeeded significantly in further removing restraints and making provisions for the flesh.

It begins with contraception. For most of human history, the greatest restraint against having sex with just anybody, anytime, was that it could produce children. Contraception promises freedom from that responsibility—offering the prospect of sex without children. But that's not enough. Contraception isn't a perfect guarantee against the conception of unwanted children. So if a child is inadvertently conceived, the culture demands the right to simply kill it. That's the high priority our world puts on the fulfillment of its lusts.

But even that is not enough of an assault on God's design. Not only does the world demand sex without children, they also want children without sex. Today, two gay men can adopt a baby.

Lesbians can even *carry* a baby. An egg fertilized by someone else can be artificially inserted into the womb. Children can be manufactured. The normal reason for marriage—a man and a woman coming together to produce children—has been completely convoluted. The family unit God designed has been utterly obviated in modern society.

Such "advancements" throw the doors wide open for endless redefinitions of what constitutes a family. These days, about forty percent of children born in the United States are born out of wedlock. But by expanding marriage to be a union between virtually anyone and *anything,* the semblance of a family no longer provides any true security or stability for children.

Not content merely to destroy the protective barrier of the family unit, society now eagerly celebrates and promotes every imaginable perversion of God's design. Homosexual marriage. Polygamy. Inscrutable transgender unions. There's nothing this world won't blasphemously label a "family."

Scripture anticipates our culture's perverse decline. Nearly two thousand years ago, Paul described the disastrous trajectory we find ourselves on today. In Romans 1, he details the consequences of sinful man's rejection of God. We've already considered how the wicked attempt to deny His creative authority, and the stupefying effect of such rebellion. But that's only the beginning. Paul continues to say: "Therefore God gave them over in the lusts of their hearts to impurity, so that their bodies would be dishonored among them" (Romans 1:24). Part of God's judgment on the world is allowing unrepentant sinners to be carried away by their lusts. Paul describes the putrefying effect of their unrestrained passions, stating,

For this reason God gave them over to degrading passions; for their women exchanged the natural function for that which is unnatural, and in the same way also the men abandoned the natural function of the woman and burned in their desire toward one another, men with men committing indecent acts and receiving in their own persons the due penalty of their error.

And just as they did not see fit to acknowledge God any longer, God gave them over to a depraved mind, to do those things which are not proper, being filled with all unrighteousness, wickedness, greed, evil; full of envy, murder, strife, deceit, malice; they are gossips, slanderers, haters of God, insolent, arrogant, boastful, inventors of evil, disobedient to parents, without understanding, untrustworthy, unloving, unmerciful; and although they know the ordinance of God, that those who practice such things are worthy of death, they not only do the same, but also give hearty approval to those who practice them. (vv. 26–32)

It's no exaggeration to say we are living at the low end of the decline described in Romans 1. We have endured the fallout of a sexual revolution (v. 24) which led to a homosexual revolution (vv. 26–27) and all the perversions that follow, to the point where our culture is now dominated by the kind of depraved, reprobate minds Paul describes. Today the world praises deviancy. They profess the nobility of degrading and destructive lifestyles. And they demand you do the same.

Not long after the Supreme Court decision to legalize same-sex marriage, I received a letter from a judge who, at the time, sat on a significant court. He explained that one of his duties was to marry people, and that the new government mandate meant that he would soon be expected to marry homosexual couples.

But he was determined that he would not participate in such blasphemous unions, and expected it would cost him his job.

I wrote him back to encourage him and thank him for his conviction. I complimented his common sense, wisdom, and astuteness in the field of law—the qualities that earned him the trust of the people and helped him rise to such a level of responsibility. And I commented on the sad irony that, because of the quality and character of his virtue, he was going to be ousted and replaced by someone who had none.

The truth is that when it comes to leading and governing our country, there is no place for those who can still think clearly. The people our country has tasked with thinking and acting for everyone else, those most responsible for our safety and well-being—the President, the members of Congress, and the Supreme Court—simply cannot think straight. The depraved, reprobate mind has ascended to the bench and to our highest seats of power.

In that sense, America may just be catching up to the rest of the world. Many countries have established so-called "hate speech" regulations to outlaw criticism or biblical clarity when it comes to homosexuality, transgenderism, and a host of other sexual perversions. For many years now in England, there have been certain topics related to biblical morality and sexuality that we are not allowed to discuss on the radio—we've had content cancelled and received fines for even mentioning the sin of homosexuality in passing on *Grace to You*. Across Western Europe, street preachers have been fined and even jailed for simply telling people what the Bible says about homosexuality. The reprobate mind has no tolerance for the biblical truth about its preferred perversions.

We're seeing another example of that playing out in Canada at the moment. A piece of legislation known as Bill C-4 passed through the Canadian parliament without opposition and took effect on January 8, 2022. The law ostensibly bans "conversion therapy" related to homosexuality and transgenderism, but the intentionally broad definitions written into the bill effectively criminalize evangelism throughout Canada.

The term "conversion therapy" specifically refers to naturalistic, therapeutic attempts to repress certain sexual desires. Such practices are often associated with pseudo-religious organizations, including some that claim to be biblically based. But the true church—and certainly the Lord of the true church—is not interested in mere behavior modification. Rather, we preach the internal transformation by the work of the Spirit through His Word. We're not merely promoting personal willpower over cognitive desires; we're pursuing true holiness through faith, repentance, and the mortification of sin.

The world does not recognize that distinction, and this new law is written in such a way that it groups together every attempt to confront or correct sinful sexual behaviors. In fact, it broadly defines "conversion therapy" as any

> practice, treatment or service designed to (a) change a person's sexual orientation to heterosexual; (b) change a person's gender identity to cisgender; (c) change a person's gender expression so that it conforms to the sex assigned to the person at birth; (d) repress or reduce non-heterosexual attraction or sexual behaviour; (e) repress a person's non-cisgender gender identity; or (f) repress or reduce a person's gender expression that does not conform to the sex assigned to the person at birth.[51]

That means simply telling someone the biblical truth about sexual sin is now a punishable crime in Canada.

The law actually goes further than that—it also prescribes that any written or recorded material that qualifies under that broad definition as conversion therapy should be categorized alongside content that "is obscene, child pornography, a voyeuristic recording, an intimate image, [or] an advertisement of sexual services."

Stunningly, turning morality on its head, the Canadian government now has declared that any gospel tracts, books, or sermon recordings that explain the biblical truth about sexual sin are just as offensive and illegal as child pornography. The law outlaws such biblical resources and teaching based on the assertion that it

> causes harm to society because, among other things, it is based on and propagates myths and stereotypes about sexual orientation, gender identity and gender expression, including the myth that heterosexuality, cisgender gender identity, and gender expression that conforms to the sex assigned to a person at birth are to be preferred over other sexual orientations, gender identities and gender expressions.

The true aim there is clear. Laws like that are not written for the protection of society. They are targeting the authority of our Creator, His Word, His design, and His people. They are attempting to outlaw biblical morality and institutionalize blasphemous corruption and flagrant sexual sin.

We know from Romans 1 the direction the world is headed. To some degree, we can anticipate and brace for its ever-declining trajectory into even more repugnant expressions of sexual deviance. We're not surprised when godless leaders steer the nation toward godless policies and ideologies. We should expect it.

But one of the great tragedies of our day is the way so many in the church have eagerly followed the course of a morally debauched culture. For decades, the world has been gradually redefining and reclassifying a long parade of gross sexual perversions—first as normal and acceptable, then as noble and praiseworthy. Many people in the church (including a large number who are in positions of leadership and influence) seem convinced that the only way to reach such a depraved culture is to capitulate to the language and even the values demanded by those who have engineered this moral upheaval. Whole churches and denominations have therefore adjusted their stance or softened their message in order to avoid conflict or criticism from a culture that tolerates everything except moral restraint. These drifting evangelicals have bought into the notion that a person's twisted sexual desires are a feature of his genetic makeup, rather than a sinful perversion he needs to be rescued from through repentance and faith in Christ. This idea in effect denies that someone caught in the clutches of sexual sin can be transformed and restored by the work of the Holy Spirit through the Word of God. It encourages people professing to believe in Christ to follow the example of the world and ground their identity in their corrupt sexual appetites.

It is probably fair to say that a majority of people in the broad evangelical movement have either embraced or are hopelessly bemused by the claim that perverted sexual desires are permanently, immutably hardwired into the souls of people who are "lesbian, gay, bisexual, transsexual, or queer/questioning" (LGBTQ+). Well-funded organizations like Revoice and Living Out have been formed specifically to defend and propagate the belief that conversion to Christ does not—indeed, *cannot*—change a person's sexual orientation. These organizations target, encourage, and give false hope to professing Christians who proudly identify as LGBTQ+. They make a point of embracing the preferred terminology of the LGBTQ+ movement and foisting it onto the church, corrupting the clarity and simplicity of God's design with the jargon of the world's increasingly ruthless sexual revolution.

All these organizations claim to be committed to a biblical view of sexual ethics, but a little investigation shows that none of them really are. Equip, for example, bills itself as "the premier consulting and training solution for churches aspiring to be places where gay Christians thrive for a lifetime according to a historic sexual ethic."[52] The designation "gay Christian" is in itself a contradiction in terms and is biblically condemnable (1 Corinthians 6:9). At their website, they define and discuss "celibate partnership," a practice common among LGBTQ+ people who profess to be Christians:

> When we at Equip use the phrase "celibate partnership", we are *specifically* describing couplings between two people of the same sex, often both same-sex attracted, and often where there is mutual attraction.... *These* celibate partnerships often involve living together, sharing a room, and even sharing a bed.... Those in *such* relationships consider themselves to be dating, refer to each other as boyfriend/girlfriend, and welcome romance into their partnership, including physical romantic activity such as making out.[53]

They do proceed to acknowledge and suggest that such partnerships "are inconsistent with spiritual friendship in Scripture, forbidden by early Church teachings, and aren't celibate." But they are iffy about whether "celibate relationships" as a whole should be considered *sinful.*\* "Unwise" is the verdict implied by the article's title ("What Are Celibate Partnerships? Are They Wise?"). And they stop short of affirming the principle Jesus taught about all desires that cannot be righteously fulfilled: "You have heard that it was said, 'You shall not commit adultery'; but I say to you that everyone who looks at a woman with lust for her has already committed adultery with her in his heart" (Matthew 5:27–28). He was, after all, simply affirming the tenth commandment, which forbids every kind of illicit desire (cf. Exodus 20:17). Jesus continued to state that sin must be radically removed rather than accommodated:

> If your right eye makes you stumble, tear it out and throw it from you; for it is better for you to lose one of the parts of your body, than for your whole body to be thrown into hell. If your right hand makes you stumble, cut it off and throw it from you; for it is better for you to lose one of the parts of your body, than for your whole body to go into hell. (Matthew 5:29–30)

So although these groups claim their view is an acceptable application of the biblical sexual ethic, by encouraging people to accept rather than mortify their sinful desires, they have actually denied the central principle of biblical sanctification—namely, that Christians are to be transformed by the renewing of their minds (Romans 12:1–2). They are instead actively campaigning for the rest of the church to acknowledge, affirm, and embrace expressions like "gay Christian" and "same-sex-attracted believer." What other kind of sin would anyone ever think is a legitimate modifier to use in identifying a disciple of Christ? Can you imagine someone wanting to be known as a Christian who

---

\* "Celibate partnerships seem unnecessarily risky to the degree that entering into one *may* constitute sin.... They are morally risky, to a degree that pursuing them at all *may* be a sin" (emphasis added).

perpetually wishes to steal, or a disciple with an insatiable desire to commit murder? Sins of the heart are illicit passions that must be put off and cast away. Scripture is not ambiguous about this. Paul says, "In reference to your former manner of life, you lay aside the old self, which is being corrupted in accordance with the lusts of deceit, and that you be renewed in the spirit of your mind" (Ephesians 4:22–23).

To smuggle the world's tolerance of sexual perversion into the church is to import a dangerous, demonic, soul-destroying doctrine. It gives people dominated by sexual sin the false assurance that God accepts them just the way they are. What many believe to be a more tolerant, loving message is actually a deceptive, destructive, diabolical lie—a deadly falsehood that is inoculating countless men and women against the transforming truth of the gospel.

Such teaching does nothing to "set [the sinner's] mind on the things above, not on the things that are on earth" (Colossians 3:2). It does nothing to help sinners "cleanse [themselves] from all defilement of flesh and spirit, perfecting holiness in the fear of God" (2 Corinthians 7:1). Rather, it makes the sinner comfortable with the very sins he is meant to put to death. It sears the conscience and stifles the work of the Spirit.

Again, such lies will lead people to hell (1 Corinthians 6:9–10), denying them the hope of true salvation and transformation. As Paul reminds us, God's church is filled with those He has rescued from the slavery of sin: "Such were some of you; but you were washed, but you were sanctified, but you were justified in the name of the Lord Jesus Christ and in the Spirit of our God" (v. 11).

The true church must faithfully and accurately tell those lost in the dominance of sexual perversion what God truly thinks of them: That because He is love, He saves unrighteous people *from* their sins. We need to plead with people in bondage to evil desires (as the Lord pleads with sinners throughout His Word) to repent and believe while there is still time. "'As I live!' declares the Lord GOD, 'I take no pleasure in the death of the wicked, but rather that the wicked turn from his way and live. Turn back, turn back from your evil ways!'" (Ezekiel 33:11).

The church cannot afford to compromise on the issue of sexual sin. God's people must be willing to tell sinners the truth about their sin, in order that we might also bring them the glorious truth about the Savior who forgives.

Our work doesn't end there. Functioning as salt and light in this world extends beyond the work of the gospel. We proclaim the good news of forgiveness and cleansing through the sacrifice of Christ. We deliver the glorious truth of His substitutionary atonement, that God "made Him who knew no sin to be sin on our behalf, so that we might become the righteousness of God in Him" (2 Corinthians 5:21). We preach freedom from sin through the sanctifying work of the Spirit. But we must also live lives that back up the truth we preach.

In particular, we need to cultivate marriages that glorify the Lord and adorn His gospel. In his letter to the Ephesians, Paul describes how God's design for marriage is a reflection of the Lord's love for His church. For the sake of our testimony to the watching world, God's people need to know and follow God's design for marriage.

Paul begins with an exhortation to wives: "Wives, be subject to your own husbands, as to the Lord. For the husband is the head of the wife, as Christ also is the head of the church, He Himself being the Savior of the body. But as the church is subject to Christ, so also the wives ought to be to their husbands in everything" (Ephesians 5:22–24).

Modern society chafes at the idea of submission, in any direction. Most think the notion of a woman submitting to her husband seems particularly outdated today, with angry dismissals of patriarchy and toxic masculinity echoing throughout our culture. Even in the church, there's a growing sentiment that biblical complementarianism is still too lopsided, and that a better balance between spouses' roles must be struck.

But that notion hinges on a fundamental misunderstanding of what Paul is actually saying here. He is not giving license for husbands to bark orders at their wives. He's not instituting chattel slavery in the home. In God's design for marriage, the husband and wife are equals, both submitting to each other in specific ways to fulfill the unique roles God has for them.

We need to break the habit of hearing the word *submission* as an automatic negative. It doesn't imply a difference in quality or a judgment of value. It's not a commentary of any kind. Rather, it's the voluntary sacrifice of oneself for another. It means willingly setting aside your own independence and priorities, and coming under God-ordained authority. And in God's design for marriage, the principle role of leadership belongs to the husband, who (in the words of this text) "is the head of the wife" (v. 23).

Don't miss that Paul instructs wives to "be subject to your *own* husbands" (v. 22). Spouses should feel a sense of ownership with one another—not in a domineering sense, but in the intimacy of their unique union. The husband and wife give themselves to each other in marriage; neither is an independent agent. They are one flesh, and they belong to one another intimately and exclusively.

We also need not imagine that submission somehow precludes the wife from intelligent participation in the life of the home. She's not meant to be distant, uninvested, or robotic.

Much less is she to be regarded as second-class or treated with condescension. As one commentator notes,

> In such submission there is nothing humiliating or degrading. It is not inconsistent with intellectual and moral and spiritual equality. It is merely the recognition of an authority which is essential to social and domestic order and welfare. It is the natural expression of love which manifests itself in willing service and finds joy in giving pleasure....
>
> Furthermore, mere listless, thoughtless subjection is not desirable if ever possible. The quick wit, the clear moral discernment, the fine instincts of a wife make of her a counselor whose influence is invaluable and almost unbounded.[54]

The counsel and companionship of a godly wife is indeed a blessing beyond measure. "House and wealth are an inheritance from fathers, but a prudent wife is from the LORD" (Proverbs 19:14).

Paul continues with an exhortation to husbands, describing their duty in God's design for marriage: "Husbands, love your wives, just as Christ also loved the church" (Ephesians 5:25). Then reflecting on the relationship between the Lord and His church, Paul highlights four ways the husband's love for his wife is manifest.

The first is *sacrificial love*. Verse 25 continues, "Husbands, love your wives, just as Christ also loved the church *and gave Himself up for her*." Most men would affirm their willingness to give up their lives for their wives, but few will be called to make such a sacrifice.

What Paul is describing here might actually be much harder for most. He's talking about dying *to self*. In other words, the husband is called and commanded to surrender his own desires and preferences when it comes to meeting his wife's needs. It's a jarring realization for many new husbands—especially those who have long been single—that life isn't just about *one's own* priorities, opinions, and satisfaction anymore. The husband is henceforth responsible for the welfare of another, and by entering into marriage he has made a covenant to provide for and prefer his wife *over* himself. The model of Christ's love for the church demands that husbands are dying to self, to live for and love their wives.

Paul describes a second way the husband is to reflect the Lord's love for His church in verses 26 and 27: "That He might *sanctify her*, having cleansed her by the washing of water with the word, that He might present to Himself the church in all her glory, having no spot or wrinkle or any such thing; but that she would be holy and blameless." Christ gave Himself for the church in order to save and sanctify His people. In the same sense, husbands are called to show *purifying love* to their wives.

Truly loving someone means wanting only what is best for that person. You can't bear for your loved one to be harmed, deceived, or corrupted. At the same time, you wouldn't lead someone you love into impurity or sinful indulgence; you wouldn't turn them over to the wickedness of the world. The husband who truly loves his wife will do everything in his power to protect his wife from sin and temptation, while encouraging her holiness and godly virtues. Loving your wife as Christ loves the church means prioritizing her purity.

The third facet of the godly husband's duty to his wife is *caring love*. Paul writes, "Husbands ought also to love their own wives as their own bodies. He who loves his own wife loves himself; for no one ever hated his own flesh, but nourishes and cherishes it, just as Christ also does the church" (vv. 28–29). In God's design, there is no separation between the husband and his wife. He cares for her just as he cares for himself.

Married men are obligated to supply what their wives need, whether it be strength, encouragement, or support—he meets her needs as best he can. God has called the husband to expend himself to protect and provide for her—and to *cherish* her. The word Paul uses refers to warming with body heat, the way a bird sits on her nest. Husbands are likewise responsible to provide a safe haven for their wives.

Finally, Paul writes, "For this reason a man shall leave his father and mother and shall be joined to his wife, and the two shall become one flesh" (v. 31). Quoting Genesis 2:24, he identifies the fourth feature of the godly husband's love for his wife: *unbreakable love*. He's emphasizing both the unity and the permanence of a godly marriage.

Husbands, can your wife rest in the security of your marriage? Make sure that she never has a reason to doubt the faithfulness of your commitment. Help her to be confident in the consistency of your love. And cultivate the mindset together that your marriage is as indivisible as the body of Christ.

God's standard for marriage has not changed. Is yours an accurate depiction of Christ's love for His church? Or is the testimony of your home tarnishing the truth of the gospel?

# CHAPTER NINE

# THE ATTACK ON WOMEN

In almost any group of people, in virtually any setting today, you could likely find someone to agree that women are under attack. But confusion and discord set in as soon as you try to identify where the attack originates, and where it is focused.

Some will argue that women are under attack in the workplace, victims of discrimination when it comes to wages and career advancement. Others will contend that the primary threat to women today lies in the realm of "reproductive rights"— that any increased limitations on their ability to murder unborn children in their wombs represents an assault on women's rights. Still others might point to more nebulous buzzwords to describe the current existential threats to women: the patriarchy, gender inequality, or toxic masculinity.

However, none of those represent the true tip of the spear when it comes to the world's attack on women. Ironically, the primary assault comes from those who are the loudest, most visible, and most insistent in declaring what they think is necessary to protect and elevate women. In reality, nothing has done more than the feminist movement to make life hard and unhappy for women.

Feminism is one of the most potent forces in modern culture. The average person might describe the movement as sensible and reasonable, working to help women secure equal pay, equal opportunities, and freedom from certain social strictures. But the true agenda behind radical feminism is chaotic, rebellious, and destructive. Our culture has been thoroughly brainwashed by feminism. As a result, marriage and the family—the primary building blocks of social and moral order—are in shambles.

Feminism fundamentally seeks to overturn the woman's God-intended function in the life of the family. What they profess as the liberation of women is actually the abandonment of the roles of wife and mother, leading to the destruction of marriage altogether. In 1971, Nancy Lehmann and Helen Sullinger authored and distributed a manifesto they dubbed "Declaration of Feminism," distributing mimeographed copies for fifty cents from a post office box in Minneapolis. Nevertheless, the document was widely circulated during a tsunami of reinvigorated feminism that swept into the culture in the aftermath of Roe v. Wade. Lehmann and Sullinger wrote with unmistakable candor:

> Marriage has existed for the benefit of men and has been a legally sanctioned method of control over women.... Male society has sold us the idea of marriage. In the past, we women have been afraid to admit that marriage wasn't all it was cracked up to be because it meant we had failed. Now we know it is the institution that has failed us and *we must work to destroy it*....
>
> The end of the institution of marriage is a necessary condition for the liberation of women. Therefore, *it is important for*

*us to encourage women to leave their husbands* and not to live individually with men.... *The nuclear family must be replaced with a new form of family.*[55] (Emphasis added)

They added this: "All of history must be written in terms of the oppression of women. We must go back to ancient female religions (like witchcraft)."[56]

In her contribution to the book *Radical Feminism*, author and activist Sheila Cronan wrote,

Wives are "owned" by their husbands in the same sense that slaves are owned by their masters—that is, that the master is entitled to free use of the slave's labor, to deny the slave his human right to freedom of movement and control over his own body....

Since marriage constitutes slavery for women, *it is clear that the Women's Movement must concentrate on attacking this institution. Freedom for women cannot be won without the abolition of marriage....*

Furthermore, marriage is the model for all other forms of discrimination against women.[57] (Emphasis added)

Obviously, feminists have no stomach for the supportive, submissive role God designed for women.

Those are not new ideas that emerged in the late twentieth century. The conflict and friction between men and women is a direct result of the Fall. In fact, it's a specific part of God's curse. "To the woman He said, 'I will greatly multiply your pain in childbirth, in pain you will bring forth children; yet your desire will be for your husband, and he will rule over you'" (Genesis 3:16). We understand that the first part of that curse is universal—

every woman suffers pain in childbirth. The second part likewise applies not only to Eve, but also to all wives in a sin-cursed world.

What did God mean when He told Eve (and wives in general) that "your desire will be for your husband"? Some have misinterpreted this as a reference to a wife's physical desire for her husband. But there's nothing wrong with sexual attraction and marital love—both are blessings and part of God's design from before the Fall (cf. Genesis 1:28). The desire mentioned here is part of the curse. It is a desire that stems from the corruption of sin, and it leads to conflict. It compels the woman's husband to rule over her. The same expression is used again in Genesis 4:7, when God speaks to Cain, warning him that "sin is crouching at the door; and its desire is for you, but you must master it." Comparing the two parallel texts, we can see that the desire mentioned in Genesis 3:16 is an urge for the woman to dominate. God is saying, in effect, "You will have a sinful desire to dominate your husband, and he is going to be forced to exercise his authority over you."

As a result of the Fall, women harbor a sinful desire to upend the divine order of authority and submission. They seek to rule over their husbands and usurp his leadership role in the family. Such conflict is a universal reality for every marriage, to one degree or another. The woman will desire control, and the man will respond with a display of dominance.

The constant effort by women to overthrow the authority of their husbands and the authority of men in the culture is a function of the curse. Feminism attempts to turn the woman's sinfully rebellious rejection of the divine order into a virtue, promising freedom, satisfaction, and fulfillment to women who overthrow male leadership.

But those are false promises that radical feminism can never fulfill. Instead, it pits women against men in constant competition, creating conflict where there should be harmony. It encourages wives to despise their own homes and their children, portraying the high calling of wife and mother as a virtual prison sentence. As they themselves have said, it causes them to view marriage as an oppressive form of slavery. That in turn leads to an epidemic of divorce and leaves women with lonely, unfulfilled lives. In the end, feminism doesn't benefit women in any of the ways it promises. It costs them everything.

The negative impact of feminism extends well beyond friction in the home and a lack of personal fulfillment. Decades of indoctrination claiming that men and women are equal in every sense has effectively erased the obvious and important differences between the two genders—and with them, many of the protections for women that were once built into the culture. Gentlemanly deference has become an insult to feminists; they take it as a sign of presumed male superiority. The radical feminists never stopped to consider how brutes and villains behave toward women when there are no gentlemen around.

Not so long ago, a man hitting a woman was unthinkable in polite society. Today it's a daily occurrence in most major cities, often in broad daylight and in full view of the public. Devoted feminists would never admit their own responsibility for increasing violence against women, but they have pushed aside many of the social restraints against it, and have left females largely unprotected.

You may recall that in the waning months of his presidency, Barack Obama issued a directive to schools across the country, instructing them to permit transgender students to use bathroom facilities that correspond to whatever gender they prefer to choose for themselves, rather than their biological sex. The instructions came along with a threat: Any schools failing to comply with the order would lose their federal funding. That directive, which was later overturned by Obama's successor, was a reaction to controversy over a state law in North Carolina that limited use of bathrooms in government buildings (including state universities) to the gender recognized at birth and recorded on the individual's birth certificate. Blinded by transgender propaganda and indifferent to the safety of women and girls, proponents of Obama's bathroom policy showed no concern about how the regulations could enable predators.

But such policies unleashed a wave of abuse. In Loudoun County, Virginia, a fourteen-year-old girl was raped in a girl's bathroom by a fellow student described as "a boy in a dress."[58] The school, Stone Bridge High School, initially intended to handle the matter internally before the police were involved and a rape kit had been administered. Not long after, in a school board meeting to promote transgender bathroom policies, the board superintendent denied that any assault had taken place in school bathrooms. Then within four months, before he had been tried on the initial charges, the "boy in a dress" assaulted another girl at a different Loudoun County high school.

Feminism has robbed the culture of the natural instinct to protect women and girls where they are most vulnerable. It foolishly refuses to see an obvious threat—like a loophole that gives predatory males unrestricted access to women's restrooms. It throws both caution and common sense to the winds. It attempts to dismiss profound matters of urgent concern, answering legitimate criticisms with nothing more than wishful thinking and willful ignorance.

Darren Agee Merager has been a registered sex offender since 2006, stemming from indecent exposure convictions in 2002 and 2003.[59] In the summer of 2021, while already facing seven further counts of indecent exposure from a separate incident in 2019, Merager again exposed himself to several female customers in a changing room at a spa in Los Angeles. A viral video of one of the outraged female customers complaining to the staff drew national attention to the incident. Merager, who claims to be a transgender woman, dismissed the complaints against him as transphobic harassment. Many people agreed, picketing outside the spa with signs that read "Stop Trans Hate" and "Trans Women Are Women."

In January of 2022, twenty-six-year-old "Hannah" Tubbs was sentenced to two years in a juvenile facility after pleading guilty to molesting a ten-year-old girl.[60] The crime took place in 2014, back when "Hannah" was known as James and was a couple months shy of his eighteenth birthday. In fact, prosecutors say he did not begin to identify as a woman until after he was taken into custody. Nevertheless, the policies of LA's liberal District Attorney George Gascon dictated that Tubbs had to be tried and sentenced as a minor, and that this predator must be jailed alongside young women like the ones he has repeatedly victimized.

Tubbs was taking advantage of new legislation in California. The Transgender Respect, Agency and Dignity Act took effect on January 1, 2021, and is intended to "allow incarcerated transgender, non-binary and intersex people to be housed and searched in a manner consistent with their gender identity."[61] The policy allows for male prisoners who identify as females to be transferred to women's prisons, regardless of their past crimes. That means a male serial rapist could be unleashed on a women's prison just because he now identifies as a woman. In response to the obvious threat this poses to incarcerated females, the state is now supplying condoms to inmates.[62]

Feminist attempts to erase the differences between men and women don't just put women in danger—they have actually set the stage for women to be eradicated altogether. Without the characteristics and qualities the culture once identified as distinctly feminine, the whole concept of what it means to be a woman has been obliterated.

The transgender movement has exploited the ensuing cultural confusion. When the word *woman* doesn't mean anything specific, it can mean anything at all.

One of the most notable and controversial nominations in the early days of the Biden presidency was Rachel Levine, who was selected to serve as the Assistant Secretary for Health in the Department of Health and Human Services. Levine became the first openly transgender person to be confirmed to federal office by the US Senate.[63] But the administration went a step further, appointing Levine a four-star admiral to oversee the US Public Health Service Commissioned Corps. The statement announcing the appointment said, "Admiral Levine now serves as the highest ranking official in the USPHS Commissioned Corps and its first-ever *female* four-star admiral" (emphasis added).[64] Levine echoed the sentiment, adopting and self-applying a term that once carried exclusive biological significance: "I am humbled to serve as the first *female* four-star officer of the U.S. Public Health Service Commissioned Corps and first openly transgender four-star officer across any of the 8 uniformed services" (emphasis added).[65] If nothing is inherently and distinctly female, anyone (or anything) can usurp the title.

Even feminists have begun to recognize the disastrous consequences of these ideologies. Here's a quote from a *New York*

*Post* article titled "Biden's trans order undoes decades of feminist progress," describing some of their well-founded concerns:

> The Biden presidency, we're told, is a historic win for women. With Kamala Harris as his Madam Vice President and a record number of women in his Cabinet, the new commander in chief is advancing the female cause....
>
> As is often the case, the gratuitous symbolic victories distract from more significant, material losses. Hours after Harris became the first female vice president, Biden signed an executive order that discriminates against her entire sex.
>
> The directive, titled "Preventing and Combating Discrimination on the Basis of Gender Identity or Sexual Orientation," spells disaster for women's shelters, sports and health care in the name of transgender equality.
>
> For instance: Institutions that receive Title IX funding must allow biological males who identify as female to compete in women's athletics. "Children should be able to learn without worrying about whether they will be denied access to...school sports," the order states.[66]

The author continues,

> Of course, by asserting that "sex" in Title IX includes "gender identity," the order not only denies reality and discriminates against biological women. It also effectively reverses Title IX, instituted to give female athletes a level playing field through female-only teams. Oh well.
>
> Biden avoids the inconvenient topic: how the bone density, muscle mass and lung capacity of female-identifying

biological males give them an unfair advantage over biological females, allowing them to unjustly claim titles, trophies and scholarships.

A few years ago in Connecticut, male high-school track-and-field athletes Terry Miller and Andraya Yearwood began competing—and consistently winning—as women. In 2020, three female track athletes filed suit against the conference policy permitting this. "My daughter would have qualified for the New England regionals in the 55-meter dash in Spring 2019," one plaintiff's mother wrote. "But instead, the top two spots went to biological boys who identify as girls."

A recent study suggests that male-to-female trans athletes retain physical advantages over their female peers even after a year of testosterone suppression. Fairness aside, this is dangerous. Recall that thanks to his male strength, trans MMA fighter Fallon Fox cracked a female opponent's skull in 2014.[67]

To mollify transgender people and activists—who demand the rest of us ignore basic biological facts and participate in their delusion—decades-old protections for women have been torn down and cast aside. As a result, women are being erased from record books and pushed aside in competitions originally intended to celebrate them and their accomplishments.

New Zealand weight lifter "Laurel" Hubbard made headlines in 2021 as the first transgender athlete to reach the Olympics. Hubbard, who had a "promising" career[68] in junior weight lifting while he was still called Gavin, was named the Sportswoman of the Year[69] by the University of Otago, despite failing to register a lift in Olympic competition.[70]

More recently, "Lia" Thomas has been shattering women's Ivy League swimming records for the University of Pennsylvania.[71]

The swimmer, formerly known as William, had spent three years on the Penn men's swimming team. His choice to identify as a woman and swim with the women's team has understandably "created an uneasy environment in the locker room, as she [sic] still retains her [sic] biologically male genitalia—which are sometimes exposed—and is attracted to women."[72] One USA Swimming official, Cynthia Millen, resigned after three decades of officiating, saying, "I can no longer participate in a sport that allows biological men to compete against women."[73] On an episode of *Tucker Carlson Tonight*, Millen explained, "The fact is that swimming is a sport in which bodies compete against bodies. Identities do not compete against identities.... Men are different from women, men swimmers are different from women, and they will always be faster than women."[74]

But transgender ideology won't allow for any differentiation between biological and transgender females. The culture's inclusive priorities demand that anyone who claims the designation must be granted it without question. One of the movement's primary rallying cries has become "Trans Women Are Women." But when pressed to define what it means to be a woman, they either can't or won't, often falling back on the postmodern trope that "It's not for me to define."

What we're left with is a culture that rebelliously refuses to acknowledge the unique qualities God imparted when He created women. These are the very features that define womanhood. But the culture today flippantly insists on applying the term to anyone who grasps for it. On the current trajectory, it won't be long before the word is entirely meaningless.

Again, if anyone or anything can be a "woman," then nothing truly is.

Perhaps the last bastion against radical feminism is the evangelical church. But it appears evangelicals may not hold their own against the feminist juggernaut much longer. Egalitarianism has been gaining ground in once-conservative evangelical circles. Following the same strategy that has conquered every other corner of society, the feminist agenda will be to erase every meaningful distinction between men and women, starting with the question of who should lead. Churches throughout the Western world are already elevating women to leadership roles that the Bible expressly reserves for men.

With much of the culture having already bought into feminism's inverted authority structure, the egalitarian agenda for the church has been very successful. Today some of the most influential voices in the church belong to women. This is in spite of the clear instructions of God's Word and the principles it sets forth for how the church should conduct itself in the world.

First Corinthians 14:35 says, "It is improper for a woman to speak in church." The word "improper" (Gk., *aischros*) was carefully chosen by the Holy Spirit to leave no lack of clarity about the force of this statement. In 1 Corinthians 11:6, the same word is translated as "disgraceful"; in Titus 1:11, it's "sordid." The point is clear—for women to usurp men for leadership offices in the church is shameful.

But why? It's true that in some circles (mostly on the fringe of the Charismatic movement) women pastors and women elders are not a new phenomenon. Some have never known a time when female leaders in the church weren't relatively commonplace. Others have heard Paul's prohibition explained away as nothing more than a first-century social norm—one that the modern church has outgrown.

God's people need to understand that His Word has not lost its relevance or its applicability. Paul's words in 1 Corinthians aren't tethered to one particular church, or one isolated era of church history. He begins his instructions against women leading in church with the words, "As in all the churches of the saints" (1 Corinthians 14:33). This is not some local restriction. It's a universal principle, applying to churches everywhere and at all times.

In its full context, the divine prohibition leaves no room for misunderstanding: "The women are to keep silent in the churches; for they are not permitted to speak, but are to subject themselves, just as the Law also says. If they desire to learn anything, let them ask their own husbands at home; for it is improper for a woman to speak in church" (vv. 34–35). The sinful heart wants to read that as unnecessarily restrictive. But believers need to understand this passage in connection with Genesis 3:16—as a guard against the rebelliousness for God-ordained authority that lives in the woman's heart since the Fall. This prohibition is actually a preventative measure against women overthrowing men as leaders in the church.

Through Paul, God is effectively telling women in the church to keep fighting their sinful desire to upend His design for authority and submission—both at home and in the church. They must subject themselves because the tendency of their fallen hearts is to rule over and dominate their husbands along with the other spiritual leaders God has placed over them. The world wants to view that kind of rebellion as noble, but we need to understand how it aids and abets the violation of God's clear standard.

Paul also makes it clear that this is not a new principle, noting, "just as the Law also says" (1 Corinthians 14:34). The order of authority and submission that God has designed for the happiness and blessing of His people reaches all the way back through His Word to creation. From the very beginning, the woman was designed as "a helper suitable for him" (Genesis 2:18). By observing the sweep of Old Testament history, we can see that pattern continue. There was never a female priest in Israel, never an authorized queen to rule over God's people. No woman was called to an ongoing prophetic role. Deborah was a judge in Old Testament Israel in a notoriously chaotic generation when men had abandoned the responsibilities of spiritual leadership. "In those days there was no king in Israel; everyone did what was right in his own eyes" (Judges 21:25). She was a living rebuke and a walking, breathing reminder of God's judgment against the spiritual passivity and the lack of courage and civic-mindedness in the men of that generation. For similar reasons, there are a few isolated instances of women who spoke prophetically (as, for example, Deborah and Anna). The scarcity of those exceptions simply underscores the fact that God's normal pattern has always been for men to have the responsibility of leadership.

Furthermore, we see throughout the Old Testament how the Lord deals with those who overthrow His ordained authority. Isaiah describes the rebellion of Gods people, and the judgment that would follow, stating, "Because the daughters of Zion are proud and walk with heads held high and seductive eyes, and go along with mincing steps and tinkle the bangles on their feet..." (Isaiah 3:16). He's depicting the rebellious hearts of the women through their behavior. They had stepped out of the God-ordained boundaries of their husbands' control, putting themselves on display for others with seduction in mind—the "mincing steps" and ornaments Isaiah describes were intended to attract the wrong kind of attention.

The subsequent verses illustrate just how far these women had gone to draw attention to themselves, rather than living in humble modesty and submission under the headship of their husbands. Isaiah writes,

> "Therefore the Lord will afflict the scalp of the daughters of Zion with scabs, and the LORD will make their foreheads bare." In that day the Lord will take away the beauty of their anklets, headbands, crescent ornaments, dangling earrings, bracelets, veils, headdresses, ankle chains, sashes, perfume boxes, amulets, finger rings, nose rings, festal robes, outer tunics, cloaks, money purses, hand mirrors, undergarments, turbans and veils. Now it will come about that instead of sweet perfume there will be putrefaction; instead of a belt, a rope; instead of well-set hair, a plucked-out scalp; instead of fine clothes, a donning of sackcloth; and branding instead of beauty. (vv. 17–24)

God would make futile the very things they had hoped to use to draw attention to themselves. Since they put such a high priority on displaying their beauty and wealth, the Lord would take it from them, leaving them bald, destitute, and ruined. It's interesting that God is so specific about the ornamentation these women employed. Nothing in that exhaustive list is wrong in itself, but the outrageous vanity and rebellion behind the rebellious women's intentions made each one an expression of sinful hearts.

But the worst of God's judgment was still to come: "Your men will fall by the sword and your mighty ones in battle" (v. 25). When women take over a culture, men become weak. When men become weak, they can be conquered. We're watching it happen in America and throughout the Western world. As more and more women ascend to power, more and more men are becoming weaker, resulting in escalating vulnerability for everyone.

These rebellious women had lived out the curse of Genesis 3. They desired to dominate their God-given authorities, and they did so to their own destruction. Verse 26 says, "And her gates"—meaning the city—"will lament and mourn, and deserted she will sit on the ground." The Lord says that once all the men have been slaughtered, these rebellious women can sit amid the rubble with all their jewelry and junk, and mourn the destruction they helped initiate. They were conquered because they overpowered their protectors. They have no one else to blame. Erroneously empowering women makes men weak. And weak men make everybody vulnerable to danger.

Earlier in the same chapter, Isaiah laments, "O My people! Their oppressors are children, and women rule over them" (v. 12). That statement isn't anti-women, in the same sense that it's not anti-children. Rather, it's illustrating the divine judgment on a nation when its men abdicate the place of authority and its young people and women rise to power. Any nation is in trouble if children are in charge. The same is true if women take control. And if you look at the United States today, you'd have to agree that men have been reduced to utter weakness as women are ascending to power.

What concerns me even more is the similar trend taking hold in the church. Young people and women have taken the lead in churches. You can see it in the sensibilities they reflect and the priorities they promote. Doctrinal depth has been forfeited in the name of emotional experiences. God's people aren't growing in the likeness of Christ and the knowledge of His Word—they're stagnating in spiritual immaturity.

The church must submit itself to God's design for authority. It must adhere to the biblical standard. Scripture is unmistakably clear: When you overthrow the divine order, the results are always disastrous.

So is there a part for women to play in God's design for the church? Of course. In his epistle to Titus, Paul describes the crucial role in which women are called to serve—a role that hinges on reverent obedience to God's Word. He says,

> Older women likewise are to be reverent in their behavior, not malicious gossips nor enslaved to much wine, teaching what is good, so that they may encourage the young women to love their husbands, to love their children, to be sensible, pure, workers at home, kind, being subject to their own husbands, so that the word of God will not be dishonored. (Titus 2:3–5)

Godly women are called to teach other women—to lead them in reverent obedience and submission to God's design for the family and the church. The kind of person Paul describes here is easy to spot, as she stands out from the crowd of worldly women. Note the contrast: She is not a gossip or a drunkard; she is known for her godly behavior.

These are women who lead by example. They set a sanctified pattern for the younger women in the church to follow. They show them what it means to love their husbands and their children. They show them how to live sensibly, how to guard against the temptations of the world, and how to glorify the Lord through their work in the home. Most of all, they display godly submission to God's authority in all areas of their lives, "so that the word of God will not be dishonored" (v. 5).

Compare that description with the kind of women in the church today who claim to be pastors and leaders. There's nothing reverent about their behavior. Their lives are neither sensible nor submissive. Purity doesn't seem like a priority. In fact, many women who routinely occupy church pulpits seem to love bawdy, ribald humor. They don't evidence a submissive love for their husbands, God-honoring devotion to their children, or their priority in the home. They've usurped authority in defiance of God and His Word. How can they claim to serve the church when they are actively dishonoring and dismissing the clear teaching of Scripture? What you fail to practice at home, you cannot effectively implement in service to the church in any capacity (cf. 1 Timothy 3:5).

Women in the church today need to understand the far-reaching implications of how they live. When they are not individually submitting to their husbands as to the Lord in marriage, and not collectively submitting to their elders in the church, God's Word is dishonored and the whole church is corrupted.

In defending the purity of the church, Paul wrote his first epistle to Timothy, "so that you will know how one ought to conduct himself in the household of God, which is the church of the living God, the pillar and support of the truth" (1 Timothy 3:15). Throughout his letter, Paul gives instructions for the life of the church. In chapter 2, he provides particular instructions for how women are supposed to conduct themselves: "Likewise, I want women to adorn themselves with proper clothing, modestly and discreetly, not with braided hair and gold or pearls or costly garments" (v. 9). That's a sharp contrast to the women described in Isaiah 3. Godly women should not be calling attention to themselves when the church gathers—they should be dressed appropriately for worship, with modesty and discretion. Paul even mentions some of the ways women of that era would draw attention to themselves, weaving pearls and gold through their braided hair to show off their wealth.

By contrast, Paul instructs godly women to adorn themselves "by means of good works, as is proper for women making a claim to godliness" (v. 10). Put simply, if you say you're a godly woman, you should be manifesting that through good works. And what are those good works? "A woman must quietly receive instruction with entire submissiveness. But I do not allow a woman to teach or exercise authority over a man, but to remain quiet" (vv. 11–12). That's how godly women are to conduct themselves in the church. They're called to modesty, discretion, good works, and submission.

Too often, we think of submission only in the negative sense— in terms of what we think we're giving up. But God's Word shows us how much He values it, and what He accomplishes through our submission. Willingly setting aside your own priorities and desires in submission to God and the authority He has placed over you is a potent testimony of your love for Him. Peter writes, "In the same way, you wives, be submissive to your own husbands so that even if any of them are disobedient to the word, they may be won without a word by the behavior of their wives, as they observe your chaste and respectful behavior" (1 Peter 3:1–2). A godly, submissive wife can win a nonbelieving husband to Christ through the testimony of her life.

Peter continues, "Your adornment must not be merely external—braiding the hair, and wearing gold jewelry, or putting on dresses; but let it be the hidden person of the heart, with the imperishable quality of a gentle and quiet spirit, which is precious in the sight of God" (vv. 3–4). It doesn't matter how dolled up you get on the outside if you're not inwardly submissive to the Lord and the authorities He has placed over you. It's the gentleness and submissiveness of your spirit that are most precious in His sight.

Peter illustrates his point from the Old Testament, saying, "For in this way in former times the holy women also, who hoped in God, used to adorn themselves, being submissive to their own husbands; just as Sarah obeyed Abraham, calling him lord, and you have become her children if you do what is right without being frightened by any fear" (vv. 5–6). That doesn't mean you need to refer to your husband as "lord"; it means you adorn yourself, the gospel, the church, and, ultimately, the Lord through the testimony of your submission. Moreover, godly women can submit "without being frightened by any fear"—they don't have to fear submitting to their husbands. They can be confident in God's design and the faithfulness of His provision.

It's no secret that women have great powers of persuasion. If they want to, they can make life pleasant or miserable for those in their sphere of influence. But the consistent message from God's Word is for them to fight the instinct of their fallen nature to reach for control and authority. There's a battle inside every marriage, every society, and every church to hold fast to the divine order, and submit to God's design for authority and submission.

You might say that sounds pretty rigid, and that's the point. You won't find a lot of wiggle room in Paul's exhortation: "A woman must quietly receive instruction with *entire submissiveness*. But I do not allow a woman to teach or exercise authority over a man, but to remain quiet" (1 Timothy 2:11–12).

But the apostle is also quick to explain that this standard is not merely his idea. "For it was Adam who was first created, and then Eve. And it was not Adam who was deceived, but the woman being deceived, fell into transgression" (vv. 13–14). Paul takes us back to Genesis 3, but this time it's to deliver a severe warning. By highlighting Eve's deception, Paul is alerting us to the fact that a woman out from under the protection of her head is vulnerable. Because of the sensibilities that are typical to women—because of their passions, their capacity for compassion, and their tendencies toward kindness, mercy, and care—they are more vulnerable to deception when unprotected. We see that played out in the culture at large today, with the vast number of women who have neither a father nor a husband to protect them from deception.

The role of women in this authority-submission partnership was designed by God in creation and confirmed in the Fall. Eve stepped out from under the protection of Adam. She was vulnerable to deception. Adam wasn't—he ate willingly, because he was bound to her in his heart. Eve sinned because she was deceived by Satan. Adam sinned because he followed her lead. He chose to abandon his authority, follow his deceived wife, and plunged the whole human race into sin. When the divine roles that God has ordained are reversed, the consequences are disastrous. Women are deceived, weak men follow, and the chaos is unending.

Where does that leave women? Are they forever saddled with the curse of Eve's sin and the fallen desire for authority they cannot have?

Paul writes, "But women will be preserved through the bearing of children if they continue in faith and love and sanctity with self-restraint" (1 Timothy 2:15). The word translated "preserved" (Gk., *sōzō*) means "saved." It doesn't mean women are granted salvation from sin through childbirth. Eternal salvation is not attainable by works; it is exclusively the gift of God by grace through faith (Ephesians 2:8–9).

Rather, Paul is describing how women are saved from the stigma of the Fall—saved from second-class status, saved from irrelevancy, and guaranteed to have a profound influence on subsequent generations. Just as Eve led the human race into sin and death, the daughters of Eve have the privilege of replenishing the population and nurturing the race in godliness through the care and guidance they give their children. This is the balance in God's design. It's not a question of superiority and inferiority—men and women simply have different roles. Women aren't called to authority, but they have an even higher calling. They bring children into the world. They get to carry, love, and nurture those little lives. They serve on the front lines of raising and discipling their children, with a depth of influence that no man will ever have. That marvelous privilege is exclusive to women.

No hulking football player ever looked into the television camera after scoring a touchdown and said, "Hi, Dad." Whenever they acknowledge their parents, it is *always* mom who gets the nod. Good mothers have the very highest position of esteem and honor.

When a mother abdicates her rightful role, the destruction is incalculable. Left to fend for himself, a child has no safe harbor amid a sea of corrupting worldly influences. There is no substitute for the guidance and care of a loving mother—there's no government entity or education system that will love that child sacrificially, no politician or pop culture figure who will put the child's needs before his own.

The attack on women is a particularly devastating feature of the war on children, because it creates an unfillable void when it pulls a mother away from what should be her first priority and highest calling.

Now, I understand that God doesn't intend for every woman to be married. There is a gift of singleness that He has bestowed on some men and women for the sake of the ministry He has set aside for them. And sometimes, for His own purposes, there are couples to whom the Lord does not grant children. But in general, God's high calling for women is for them to have children and to pour their lives into those little souls. He has given them the greatest of all influence to execute "in faith and love and sanctity with self-restraint" (1 Timothy 2:15).

I'm grateful to say I know many women like that. God has blessed the church I pastor with strong men who love His truth and vigorously defend the faith. But those who display grace and hospitality the most—and who stand out to those who visit— are the women. Their sweetness, kindness, tenderheartedness, goodness, mercy, and love permeate our church and bless every member.

Every church needs strong men. But the heart and soul of a good church are the precious, godly women who live their lives in faith, love, sanctity, and self-restraint, raising godly children and supporting the work of the Word throughout the church. God grant us more women like that.

# CHAPTER TEN

# THE ATTACK ON MEN

The assaults from the radical feminist movement are not limited to their attack on women. While feminists have managed to elevate women to levels of authority and leadership God never intended—covertly robbing them of the blessed role for which He specifically designed women in the first place—feminism's *overt* attack on men is just as crucial to their satanic agenda. They first have to strip men of their authority, leadership, and responsibility before they can foist those roles illegitimately on women.

For decades, they have been doing just that.

You can see how effective they have been virtually everywhere you look. Western society has relegated men to the trash heap. They have declared masculinity itself "toxic." Now the culture is engaged in an all-out assault against distinctly masculine qualities. Assertiveness is presumed to be arrogance; independence is mistaken for selfishness. Strength and courage are taken as aggression; leadership as heavy-handed dominance. The familiar features of manhood are seen as a threat to society at large—symptoms of a disease that must be mitigated, if not cured altogether.

Masculinity itself is in the crosshairs. Manhood has been marginalized. Men are treated as villains, especially if they refuse to renounce every vestige of manly toughness, courage, and strength in order to adopt more effeminate characteristics.

Indeed, the postmodern world rejects the idea of gender norms—that some characteristics are inherently feminine and others inherently masculine. They'll argue vigorously that biology has nothing to do with those characteristics, that gender norms are merely a social construct that the male-dominated culture has imposed throughout the centuries—and that's why masculinity is inherently toxic. The attack on manhood is perhaps the most overt, oppressive, and angry assault in the continuing effort to erase every distinction between men and women. And in the relentless war on children, it has been one of the most destructive, because it has literally left millions of children to grow up without any strong, protective father figures, and it eliminates the masculine role models young boys need.

So we're not supposed to recognize masculine virtues. On the other hand, it is okay to recognize the qualities of traditional manhood *if* the point is to condemn and marginalize those traits.

Nevertheless, even the most radical feminists struggle to define what they mean when they speak of "toxic masculinity." Many will insist that they don't mean every characteristic that has been traditionally deemed "manly" is toxic. But when they describe what they are aiming for, it is clear that they want men to be just like women. An article at the *Medical News Today* website, for example, acknowledges that definitions attempting to detail what is supposedly toxic about masculinity are fluid. And as that expression has gained traction in public discourse, more and more of the character qualities traditionally deemed "masculine" are now being put in the "toxic" category. "The notion of toxic masculinity centers on the idea that some masculinity traits are archaic," they say.[75] This evidently includes manly qualities like strength, emotional stability, and other character traits usually associated with maturity and leadership. In the words of the article,

> The exact definition of toxic masculinity has evolved over time....

> In modern society, people often use the term toxic masculinity to describe exaggerated masculine traits that many cultures have widely accepted or glorified.

> This harmful concept of masculinity also places significant importance on "manliness" based on:
> - strength
> - lack of emotion
> - self-sufficiency
> - dominance
> - sexual virility

> .... Overemphasis of these traits may lead to harmful imbalances in someone trying to live up to these expectations.[76]

The article goes on to characterize expressions like "man up" and "boys will be boys" as deeply misogynistic.

When you refuse to acknowledge the realities of sin and total depravity, you're forced to concoct alternative explanations for the corruption that dominates this world. In the wake of several high-profile sex scandals, the culture needed somewhere to lay the blame for the wickedness and immorality of powerful men. But it couldn't be a feature common to everyone. They needed a flaw they could identify and isolate, absolving themselves in the process. The expression "toxic masculinity" allows an increasingly feminized culture to distance itself from the diagnosis.

But it didn't end with explaining away deviant and abusive behavior. "Toxic masculinity" is an intentionally broad term—broad enough to encompass virtually anything the world finds objectionable about men and traditional manhood. In 2019, the American Psychological Association published its *Guidelines for Psychological Practice With Boys and Men*, which "draw on more than 40 years of research showing that *traditional masculinity is psychologically harmful* and that socializing boys to suppress their emotions causes damage that echoes both inwardly and outwardly" (emphasis added).[77] In the eyes of modern psychology, traditional masculinity is even a threat to your health.

Here's how the experts determined there was a problem in the first place:

> Something is amiss for men.... Men commit 90 percent of homicides in the United States and represent 77 percent of homicide victims. They're the demographic group most at risk of being victimized by violent crime. They are 3.5 times more likely than women to die by suicide, and their life expectancy is 4.9 years shorter than women's. Boys are far more likely to be diagnosed with attention-deficit hyperactivity disorder than girls, and they face harsher punishments in school—especially boys of color.[78]

So the whole attempt to marshal and marginalize masculinity developed from carefully observing the fact that there *are indeed* significant distinctions between men and women. They continued: "Once psychologists began studying the experiences of women through a gender lens, it became increasingly clear that the study of men needed the same gender-aware approach....

The main thrust of the subsequent research is that traditional masculinity—marked by stoicism, competitiveness, dominance and aggression—is, on the whole, harmful."[79]

So there is no mistaking the agenda—this is an attempt to redefine what it means to be a man. With the concept of toxic masculinity so vague and ill-defined, proponents can point the word "toxic" like a weapon toward virtually any masculine characteristic they want to destroy. But consider the kind of examples that are invoked to suggest that male strength is bad—things like bullying, catcalling, and violent aggression. Those are not features of traditional masculinity; a man can exhibit strength, competitiveness, and leadership ability without being guilty of any of those evils. To suggest that such sins stem automatically from masculine characteristics is to play a shell game with the real issues. Mean-spirited misdeeds like browbeating, cruelty, oppression, and a pugnacious demeanor are expressions of sin, not true manhood.

But the point of feminist rhetoric against masculinity is to caricature all men who exhibit manliness as abusive. Any culture convinced that masculinity is the problem—even a threat to health—will eagerly embrace whatever redefinition gets put forward. As conservative commentator Ben Shapiro puts it, "The whole point here is to rob masculinity of its masculine side.... The point is to redefine masculinity to now include doing feminine things."[80] That is exactly right. It's not merely a question of whether boys should be more emotional and less stoic or competitive. The real agenda is to redefine what it means to be a man. Shapiro explains,

> Feminizing males is not the goal of being masculine. *Masculine* and *feminine* have definitions. It is good for men to

be masculine. It is a good thing to train boys to be masculine—and then, for masculinity to be tempered by civilization. For all of human history, masculinity unbound has had very, very negative effects—masculinity unbound from anything like responsibility. The aggressive instinct that is inherent in males, generally speaking, unbound from civilization and civilizing influences and traditional Judeo-Christian morality, has had dire, dire effects.

But masculinity has also done incredibly great things for the world. Assertiveness has meant progress. Assertiveness has meant growth. Assertiveness has meant defense of family and hearth and home. It has meant prosperity. Masculinity is a good thing for civilizations. And civilizations that decide to essentially defenestrate masculinity are going to bear some pretty ill effects.[81]

If the true goal were merely to mitigate aggressive, violent behavior among males, we would be emphasizing how to raise boys and young men with a proper sense of right and wrong—how to instill moral values in them. And frankly, we'd be talking about the vital importance of having a father in the home in the first place. We would have to acknowledge the devastation that has been unleashed in our society by generations of fatherless children. Instead, our society has rejected the social value of true manhood. Shapiro continues,

Masculinity is a good and important thing when channeled properly. It requires men to defend family. It requires men to provide. It requires men to channel their aggressive instincts toward defense of values and civilization.... When you make men more feminine, when you suggest that men need to be like women...this undermines some fundamentally good thing about men. In the same way that if you said that women ought to act like men—it's funny, if you say that women ought to act more like men, this is considered sexist *because it actually is sexist*. But if you say that men ought to act more like women, this is considered progressive and forward thinking.[82] (Emphasis added)

There's an element of self-fulfilling prophecy in all this. The culture practically invites young men to not grow up. Some can hold onto immaturity well into their thirties and forties—some further. They're not taking on responsibilities, they're not providing for their families, and they're of no real benefit to society. In that sense, they're not truly men.

With a dearth of true men in our society—men who will defend and protect those who need it—we're facing an onslaught of sinful, unrestrained males who are seizing on the weakness of a passive, feminized culture. Their unrestrained aggression and violence confirms to the world that the real problem is traditional masculinity.

The truth is we don't need less masculinity. We need more *men*.

Perhaps nowhere is that pressing need more apparent than in the modern evangelical church. For the past five decades or longer, some of the largest and most influential churches in America have followed a philosophy of ministry that is more entertaining than instructive. To this day, every list of the largest churches in the nation is dominated if not completely monopolized by churches where you're far more likely to hear a moralistic message exegeting the latest Hollywood blockbuster than you are to hear a real sermon with biblical content. Thousands of adults have spent their entire Christian life in churches dominated by a pragmatic ministry philosophy. Boosting attendance takes priority over teaching, reproof, correction, and training in righteousness (2 Timothy 3:16). Their leaders have not been faithful to insure "that the man of God may be equipped, having been thoroughly equipped [through the work of God's Word] for every good work" (2 Timothy 3:17, LSB). Therefore, countless evangelicals who are now adults, even those serving in positions of church leadership, have never really known any style of church ministry that isn't tantamount to a pep rally. Church for them has been like a perpetual youth group that is designed chiefly to amuse rather than edify. No wonder they haven't attained true manhood. No wonder they are like "children, tossed here and there by waves and carried about by every wind of doctrine, by the trickery of men, by craftiness in deceitful scheming" (Ephesians 4:14).

That quotation comes from the same context where the apostle defines as simply as possible what constitutes true manhood. "A mature man," Paul says, is someone who seeks to attain "the measure of the stature which belongs to the fullness of Christ" (v. 13). Christlikeness is real manhood. It includes several of the very qualities that have been labeled "toxic" by postmodern feminists—features like strength, courage, steadfastness, authority, and leadership—all expressed both firmly and lovingly. It is a standard that none of us can attain perfectly, but the fact that men can (and do) misuse their strength to abuse or oppress is no reason to conclude that manly strength is a vice rather than a virtue. Nor is society's growing contempt for manhood a reason for Christian men to become womanly. We must "press on toward the goal for the prize of the upward call of God in Christ Jesus" (Philippians 3:14).

What specific things does God's Word single out as the marks of mature manhood? What are the goals every Christian man should be working toward?

In 1 Timothy 3, Paul lays out the biblical qualifications for pastors and elders. And while not all Christian men are called to the highest levels of church leadership, these qualities are nonetheless marks of spiritual maturity and godliness. Even if you have no desire to serve as an elder in your church, you still should seek to meet these qualifications. These are the characteristics that define a godly, mature, truly manly life. In effect, this is God's description of godly manhood:

> An overseer, then, must be above reproach, the husband of one wife, temperate, prudent, respectable, hospitable, able to teach, not addicted to wine or pugnacious, but gentle, peaceable, free from the love of money. He must be one who manages his own household well, keeping his children under control with all dignity (but if a man does not know how to manage his own household, how will he take care of the church of God?), and not a new convert, so that he will not become conceited and fall into the condemnation incurred by the devil. And he must have a good reputation with those outside the church, so that he will not fall into reproach and the snare of the devil. (1 Timothy 3:2–7)

Paul wanted Timothy to understand what kind of men he should be looking for to help lead the Ephesian church—the kind of men who are fit for the work of ministry and spiritual leadership. Men, if true masculine maturity is your goal, these are the qualities you need to be cultivating in your own life.

The first qualification in Paul's list is that the godly man "must be above reproach" (v. 2). It means there is no accusation that can be brought against him regarding sin in his life. There are no obvious faults or flaws visible to those who observe him—there's nothing about the pattern of his life that could bring a reproach on him, his Lord, or his church.

That doesn't mean he won't sin; it means that he keeps short accounts when he does. He confesses his sins and makes restitution where it's needed so that he doesn't develop a bad reputation or seem indifferent to God's righteous standard. The godly man is constantly weeding out the sin in his life because he does not want to blight the testimony of the Savior or His truth.

God's men understand that the world is always looking for hypocrisy in the church—that sinners want to excuse and legitimize their unbelief. So they conduct themselves in such a way that their lives adorn the gospel, not tarnish it. They live diligent and disciplined lives, guarding their minds and their steps, so that nothing they do can bring a reproach against Christ. That's how Paul described his own pursuit of godliness:

> Do you not know that those who run in a race all run, but only one receives the prize? Run in such a way that you may win. Everyone who competes in the games exercises self-control in all things. They then do it to receive a perishable wreath, but we an imperishable. Therefore I run in such a way, as not without aim; I box in such a way, as not beating the air; but I discipline my body and make it my slave, so that, after I have preached to others, I myself will not be disqualified. (1 Corinthians 9:24–27)

In other words, being above reproach isn't a one-time achievement. It's a lifestyle the godly man has to cultivate. Paul describes the features of that lifestyle in the qualifications that follow. Everything else in the list of qualifications for eldership is an explanation of what it means to be above reproach.

Paul says next that the godly man must be "the husband of one wife" (1 Timothy 3:2). He is not making the man's marital status the issue. Nor is this merely a prohibition against polygamy. The Greek expression consists of three words that simply mean "man," the numeral "one," and "woman"—literally, "a one-woman man." This has to do with the purity of his moral character more than his marital status. Is he the kind of man who is faithfully and solely devoted to one woman?

Remember that marital faithfulness is not limited to a man's outward behavior. To harbor secret desires for a woman or women other than one's wife is a sinful lust no better than same-sex attraction. It is an evil to be mortified. As Christ said in the Sermon on the Mount, "Everyone who looks at a woman with lust for her has already committed adultery with her in his heart" (Matthew 5:28). And the principle applies to single men as well as husbands. A godly man is not to have carnal desires for women to whom he is not married.

Much like the corruption and immorality that dominate our culture, sexual sin was rampant in Ephesus. That city was home to a lewd statue of the Roman goddess Diana. Most if not all of the believers in that church had been saved out of a particularly perverse kind of idolatry. But God was gracious to them, as He is to believers today, washing and redeeming us from lives of unrepentant sin. He can transform the foulest sinner. He can breathe life into those dead in their sins. As Paul wrote, "If anyone is in Christ, he is a new creature; the old things passed away; behold, new things have come" (2 Corinthians 5:17). No matter what kind of life you lived before Christ, you have been made alive in Him through repentance and faith, transformed and renewed by the Spirit working through His Word. You may still bear the scars of your former sins, but by God's grace you can be a one-woman man.

The next qualification on Paul's checklist is translated as "temperate" (1 Timothy 3:2). The Greek word *nēphalion* literally means "without wine." That's not to say that godly men must be teetotalers. Scripture is clear about the medicinal benefits of wine. In this same epistle, Paul will exhort Timothy, "No longer drink water exclusively, but use a little wine for the sake of your stomach and your frequent ailments" (5:23). Proverbs 31:6 says, "Give strong drink to him who is perishing, and wine to him whose life is bitter."

Rather, Paul is referring to sobriety in contrast to intoxication. Wine was commonplace in the New Testament world. Most often, it was significantly diluted with water. But even then, intoxication was still a threat. In the words of Proverbs 20:1, "Wine is a mocker, strong drink a brawler, and whoever is intoxicated by it is not wise." Throughout the Old Testament, God issued warnings to His servants to abstain from drinking. The priests were forbidden from drinking before they served in the Tabernacle (Leviticus 10:9). Rulers were admonished not to drink, lest it impair their judgment (Proverbs 31:4–5).

In the same way, godly men need to protect the mental faculties the Lord has blessed them with. It's not merely about abstaining from intoxication. They must avoid excess of any kind that dulls their senses or inhibits their ability to be alert, think clearly, and exercise sound judgment. For some, overeating can be just as detrimental as drinking. Godly men understand those dangers and avoid excess in all its forms. Describing that kind of self-discipline, William Hendriksen wrote, "His pleasures are not primarily those of the sense...but those of the soul."[83] The church has an urgent need for such men today.

Temperance leads to another characteristic of godly men—Paul says they are also "prudent" (1 Timothy 3:2). Because he is not given to excess, the godly man knows how to guard and govern his mind. He has the right priorities. In a word, he is self-disciplined.

It's remarkable how many men reach adulthood these days without growing out of the whimsy and frivolity of childhood. The prudent man isn't subject to his emotions or the whims of the flesh; he's steady. That doesn't mean he's cold, robotic, and humorless. It means his lighter side is tempered by the truth about sin and a lost world bent on disobedience to God. He's not silly when it comes to spiritual matters. He takes serious issues seriously, rightly appraising the world and its corrupting influences.

The prudent man embodies Paul's exhortation to the Philippians. Paul says, "Finally, brethren, whatever is true, whatever is honorable, whatever is right, whatever is pure, whatever is lovely, whatever is of good repute, if there is any excellence and if anything worthy of praise, dwell on these things" (Philippians 4:8). His mind is devoted to God's truth, and subject to the supremacy of Christ.

While prudence guides the way a godly man thinks, Paul identifies the way he lives as "respectable" (1 Timothy 3:2). The Greek word *kosmios* connotes a sense of orderliness. God's men don't live haphazard, chaotic lives. They don't leave a slew of disorganized plans and unaccomplished goals in their wake. Rampant disorder doesn't reflect a life (or a mind) devoted to God and His truth.

The godly man's lifestyle isn't dominated by chaos—just the opposite. His self-disciplined mind leads to a respectable, well-organized life.

Paul says the godly man's life is further marked out by how he treats strangers—that he must be "hospitable" (v. 2). But this isn't just a question of how well he treats his friends. The idea here has to do with showing love to strangers.

Frankly, it is easy to show hospitality to those with whom you already have a close relationship—or those with whom you want to cultivate a closer one. But that kind of hospitality isn't sacrificial. As the Lord instructed His followers, "When you give a luncheon or a dinner, do not invite your friends or your brothers or your relatives or rich neighbors, otherwise they may also invite you in return and that will be your repayment. But when you give a reception, invite the poor, the crippled, the lame, the blind, and you will be blessed, since they do not have the means to repay you; for you will be repaid at the resurrection of the righteous" (Luke 14:12–14).

Hospitality does not require a blithe indifference to your own safety or that of your family. The Lord's exhortation in Matthew 10:16 still applies: "Behold, I send you out as sheep in the midst of wolves; so be shrewd as serpents and innocent as doves." It's not safe to welcome just anyone into your home or your vehicle. Nevertheless, while not setting aside our wisdom or our duty to protect our families, we need to seek to show kindness and care for those who need it. As the writer of Hebrews reminds us, "Do not neglect to show hospitality to strangers, for by this some have entertained angels without knowing it" (Hebrews 13:2).

Since we're considering Paul's list of qualifications as the measure of godly manhood, we won't spend much time on the next one—"able to teach"—because it is the only one that is specific to elders and pastors.† But it's worth noting that "able to teach" isn't just referring to a skill or talent. These are still moral qualifications that Paul is describing. The point is the quality of a

† You can find a thorough exposition of 1 Timothy 3 in *The MacArthur New Testament Commentary: 1 Timothy* (Chicago: Moody, 1995).

man's teaching must be bolstered by the quality of his life. In the words of Richard Baxter, "He that means as he speaks will surely do as he speaks."[84]

In 1 Timothy 3:3, Paul continues to unpack the qualities that delineate a godly man. Another key feature of his reputation is that he is "not addicted to wine." Of course we understand that a drunk would not be considered "above reproach" (v. 2), nor would he qualify as an elder or pastor. Perhaps the better translation of the word Paul uses here (Gk., *paroinos*) is simply "one who drinks." But the apostle already identified the importance of temperance and how the godly man must avoid intoxication or any other kinds of excess that would inhibit his ability to lead. What different facet of a man's reputation is Paul referring to here?

While temperance has to do with a man's intake, this has more to do with his associations. The godly man is not at home in bars and taverns—he doesn't partake in the raucous, noisy events that commonly accompany drinkers. It's not merely that he stops short of intoxication. He doesn't associate with the intoxicated. This qualification has to do with the kind of characters he surrounds himself with, and the quality of the example he sets for the rest of God's people.

Paul immediately follows with another prohibitive qualification. Just as God's men are not to associate with drinkers and drunkenness, they must also not be "pugnacious" (v. 3). In simple terms, he is not one who looks to settle things with his fists. Short tempers and needless violence are not features of biblical manhood. A true man is strong, but he is not a brawler. While such things mistakenly pass for masculinity in the world, the godly man understands the example he needs to set for those watching how he conducts himself.

And while there may come a time when he is forced to get physical, the godly man does everything he can to handle situations with a cool head and a calm spirit. As Paul reminded Timothy in a subsequent letter, "The Lord's bond-servant must not be quarrelsome, but be kind to all...[and] patient when wronged" (2 Timothy 2:24).

By contrast, Paul says the godly man is "gentle" (1 Timothy 3:3). This term encompasses several characteristics—it means he is considerate, gracious, genial, and forbearing. He is the kind of person who remembers the good and forgets the bad. He is quick to pardon the failures of others—especially those who have failed him. In the words of 1 Corinthians 13:5, he "does not take into account a wrong suffered."

That kind of gentleness is a rare commodity today. The modern man excels at keeping score, even with those closest to him. But that kind of behavior is a cancer to the church. God's people are still flawed and fallen. Christians are going to sin against one another. But godly men discipline themselves to not dwell on how they have been let down or disappointed. They're gracious and gentle with those around them, understanding that they also require forgiveness and patience from others.

Paul further drives home that point with the next characteristic in his list: "peaceable" (1 Timothy 3:3). The literal idea is that the godly man is reluctant to fight. Unlike the prohibition against pugnacious men, this has more to do with being contentious and argumentative. The godly man is not given to quarrelling. Yes, he will "contend earnestly for the faith" (Jude 3), but he's not out to pick fights on the basis of opinions and preferences.

Rather, the godly man embodies Paul's exhortation, "If possible, so far as it depends on you, be at peace with all men"

(Romans 12:18). He is willing to die to self to protect unity and harmony—particularly among God's people.

Verse 3 concludes with one more qualification: The godly man should be "free from the love of money." He cannot be greedy or obsessed with financial ambitions. He guards his heart from the corrupting love of worldly things, understanding how "the earth-bound desires of a covetous spirit always clip the wings of faith and love."[85]

God's men need to heed Paul's warning words to his ministry apprentice:

> But godliness actually is a means of great gain when accompanied by contentment. For we have brought nothing into the world, so we cannot take anything out of it either. If we have food and covering, with these we shall be content. But those who want to get rich fall into temptation and a snare and many foolish and harmful desires which plunge men into ruin and destruction. For the love of money is a root of all sorts of evil, and some by longing for it have wandered away from the faith and pierced themselves with many griefs. (1 Timothy 6:6–10)

During his own ministry in the Ephesian church, Paul assured the leaders, "I have coveted no one's silver or gold or clothes" (Acts 20:33). Likewise, the godly man is content with all the blessings the Lord has given him, while understanding that his true riches are in heaven.

Paul highlights another key proving ground for a man's godly qualities in 1 Timothy 3:4–5: "He must be one who manages his own household well, keeping his children under control with all dignity (but if a man does not know how to manage his own household, how will he take care of the church of God?)."

Certainly some of the other qualities we've already discussed will be on display in how a man manages his home. You'll know if he is self-disciplined and well organized. Through his relationships with his wife and children, you'll see whether he is gentle and peaceable. You'll see if he is truly hospitable, and if he is free from the love of money.

But Paul highlights other qualities that will be borne out in his home life. The question of whether he "manages his own household well" has to do with his stewardship. It's not just a question of avoiding covetousness and the love of money. How has the Lord blessed him, and what kind of steward is he with those blessings?

And it's not just a question of how he manages *financial* blessings. What kind of father is he? How well do his children behave? A man's ability to keep "his children under control with all dignity" speaks to the consistency and integrity of his life. An individual can put on a convincing show of godliness if all you ever see is how he carries himself in public. Children are not as capable of keeping up the façade. How a man's children behave is a strong indicator of his priorities and how he spends his time. Do his children bring honor to their parents, or has he failed to raise them with a sense of respect and discipline?

The quality of a man's home life speaks to the integrity of the other godly characteristics in Paul's list. They'll either be verified in his home, or the disparity between his public and private life will call into question whether he truly possesses these godly qualities in the first place.

In verse 6, Paul adds, "And not a new convert, so that he will not become conceited and fall into the condemnation incurred by the devil." This qualification has specific implications for pastors and elders in the church. But it's also worth considering how it applies within our focus on these qualities as the measure of godliness. As we've already seen, the evangelical church is overrun with immature believers—and specifically men who don't know their Bibles, don't adhere to sound doctrine, and don't seem to care. They're content with shallow faith and weak teaching. They're happy to have their ears tickled. Such spiritual laziness flies in the face of the godly characteristics Paul emphasizes in 1 Timothy. Whatever other qualities they might seem to possess, there is no substitute for spiritual maturity.

There's another quality implied in verse 6; Paul identifies spiritual maturity as a necessity "so that he will not become conceited and fall into the condemnation incurred by the devil." Humility is a fundamental aspect of true godliness, and is often proportional to a believer's spiritual maturity. While the new believer might be tempted to think highly of himself and his giftedness, a mature believer recognizes the flesh that still remains and the sin he has yet to mortify. Paul is a good example of how humility and spiritual maturity go hand in hand. Earlier in his letter to Timothy, Paul, who considered himself "the least of the apostles, and not fit to be called an apostle" (1 Corinthians 15:9), went even further and referred to himself as the "foremost of all [sinners]" (1 Timothy 1:15). The godly man cultivates that same sense of humility, understanding the danger of pride.

Finally, Paul writes, "And he must have a good reputation with those outside the church, so that he will not fall into reproach and the snare of the devil" (1 Timothy 3:7). It's not enough for the godly man to have a good reputation within his family and his church—weight must also be given to how he is viewed in the world. In some ways, we have returned to the idea of being above reproach—how is he known in the world, and what is he known for? Is he a different person altogether in the world's eyes? Is he marked by compromise and capitulation? Or is his reputation consistent regardless of where he is and with whom he interacts?

Note that a good reputation is not the same thing as being beloved and embraced by the world. Believers should count on facing opposition from the world. Christ told His people to expect the world's outright contempt: "If the world hates you, you know that it has hated Me before it hated you. If you were of the world, the world would love its own; but because you are not of the world, but I chose you out of the world, because of this the world hates you" (John 15:18–19). Frankly, if you're not facing some kind of opposition from the world, it's worth asking if your life is distinctly Christlike.

But it's a different thing entirely if we lose the respect of the world because of some sin or inconsistency between our profession of faith and our behavior. Having "a good reputation with those outside the church" is about the integrity and consistency of the man's life. The godly man is the same man wherever he goes. There are no shades or versions of him, depending on his surroundings. In short, he's not a hypocrite. All the various eyes observing the godly man's life see the same thing. The consistency of his reputation is unassailable.

May God raise up a generation of such men for the sake of His church and the work of His kingdom.

# EPILOGUE

There is hope!

Though this war is diabolical, there can be triumph when we train our children in the ways of the Lord.

God knew that war on children would be the devil's strategy, so He gave Israel guidance to fight this battle. Moses commanded the parents of Israel: "You shall teach [the ways of God] diligently to your sons and shall talk of them when you sit in your house and when you walk by the way and when you lie down and when you rise up" (Deuteronomy 6:7). God's intent for our children is for them to be clad with the full armor of God's Word. And we can trust God that this instruction will be fruitful. Proverbs affirms, "Train up a child in the way he should go, even when he is old he will not depart from it" (Proverbs 22:6).

As a Christian parent, you cannot sit back and passively watch this world take your child's heart captive and enslave him or her to a godless ideology. You must recognize this world's cunning tactics and respond with conviction. This is a full-fledged spiritual war for the soul of your child. You must understand that your child is the target of this war. This world is concertedly laboring to move your child from being under your influence to being under their indoctrination.

Since the fall of Adam and Eve, Satan has been diligently at work to make this a difficult battle for parents. He has been assaulting the God-ordained duties of men and women to dismantle the family. And with no shortage of success—especially now in America—his focus has become our children. With broken families now the norm in the nation, the home that God intended to be the haven of instruction and discipline offers no such hope. The only hope is to fulfill the role that God has designed for each father and mother, and to raise your child in the Word of God.

God has called all His children to provide refuge for their children in this hostile world.

# ENDNOTES

1 Karen D'Souza, "Universal preschool and affordable child care: What survives in Biden's spending bill," Early Learning, *EdSource*, November 19, 2021, https://edsource.org/2021/universal-preschool-and-affordable-child-care-what-survives-in-bidens-spending-bill/663945.

2 Ingrid Jacques, "Who knows what's best for kids? Hint: Biden and Democrats don't think it's parents," Opinion, *USA Today*, April 27, 2023, https://www.usatoday.com/story/opinion/columnist/2023/04/27/biden-government-dictate-kids-education-schools-not-parents/11743676002.

3 C-SPAN, "Vice President Harris Remarks on Mental Health and Wellness," May 23, 2022, https://www.c-span.org/video/?520516-1/vice-president-harris-remarks-mental-health-wellness.

4 Joshua Rhett Miller, "Disney exec vows more gay characters amid huge inclusivity push," News, *New York Post*, March 30, 2022, https://nypost.com/2022/03/30/disney-executive-wants-more-lgbtqia-minority-character/.

5 Randall O'Bannon, "62,502,904 Babies Have Been Killed in Abortions
Since Roe v. Wade in 1973," National, *LifeNews.com*, January 18,
2021, https://www.lifenews.com/2021/01/18/62502904-babies-
have-been-killed-in-abortions-since-roe-v-wade-in-1973.

6 E. E. Carpenter, "Sacrifice, Human," *The International Standard Bible
Encyclopedia*, revised edition (Grand Rapids: Eerdmans, 1979–
1988), 4:258–60.

7 "Ancient Carthaginians really did sacrifice their children," University
of Oxford, *News and Events*, January 23, 2014,
https://www.ox.ac.uk/news/2014-01-23-ancient-carthaginians-real-
ly-did-sacrifice-their-children; and see Betsy Reed, "Carthaginians
sacrificed own children, archaeologists say," *Guardian US*, January
21, 2014,
https://www.theguardian.com/science/2014/jan/21/carthagin-
ians-sacrificed-own-children-study#:~:text=The%20Roman%20
historian%20Diodorus%20and,into%20a%20sort%20of%20gaping.

8 Johann Joseph Ignaz von Döllinger, *Judenthum und Heidenthum*,
i. 427, English translation, cited in George Rawlinson, *History of
Phoenicia* (London: Longmans, Green, 1889), 347.

9 Diodorus Siculus, *Library of History*, trans. Russel M. Geer, 12 vols.
(Cambridge, MA: Harvard, 1954), 10:181–82.

10 Much later in modern Jewish history, the girls were inducted as
daughters of the law at their *bat mitzvah*. Ronald L. Eisenberg,
*The JPS Guide to Jewish Traditions* (Philadelphia: The Jewish
Publication Society, 2004), 23–27.

11 Lucius Annaeus Seneca, "On Anger," *Seneca: Moral and Political
Essays*, ed. John M. Cooper and J. F. Procope (Cambridge, MA:
Cambridge University Press, 1995), 15.

12 Dorothy Law Nolte, *Children Live What They Learn* (New York:
Workman, 1998), vi–vii.

13 "What Would the World Look like If NOT Having Kids Was the Cultural Norm?: Less stress, less heartache, less judgment. And we
hate this idea...why?" *Medium*, August 16, 2023,
https://medium.com.

14 James Gallagher, "Fertility rate: 'Jaw-dropping' global crash in children being born," Health, *BBC News*, July 15, 2020, https://www.bbc.com/news/health-53409521.

15 Ibid.

16 Gretchen Livingston, "Is U.S. fertility at an all-time low? Two of three measures point to yes," *Pew Research Center*, May 22, 2019, https://www.pewresearch.org/short-reads/2019/05/22/u-s-fertility-rate-explained/.

17 Brady E. Hamilton, Joyce A. Martin, and Michelle J. K. Osterman, "Births: Provisional Data for 2020," Report No. 012, *NVSS Vital Statistics Rapid Release*, May 2021, https://www.cdc.gov/nchs/data/vsrr/vsrr012-508.pdf.

18 Gretchen Livingston, "Is U.S. fertility at an all-time low? Two of three measures point to yes," *Pew Research Center*, May 22, 2019, https://www.pewresearch.org/short-reads/2019/05/22/u-s-fertility-rate-explained/.

19 Leah MarieAnn Klett, "More adults say they're not planning to have children amid declining birth rates, poll finds," News, *Christian Post*, November 26, 2021, https://www.christianpost.com/news/more-adults-say-theyre-not-planning-to-have-children-poll-finds.html.

20 Richard Fry, Jeffrey S. Passel, and D'verah Cohn, "A majority of young adults in the U.S. live with their parents for the first time since the Great Depression," Pew Research Center, September 4, 2020, https://www.pewresearch.org/short-reads/2020/09/04/a-majority-of-young-adults-in-the-u-s-live-with-their-parents-for-the-first-time-since-the-great-depression/.

21 Aila Slisco, "Woman Allegedly Breastfeeds Cat on Delta Airlines Flight," News, *Newsweek*, November 26, 2021, https://www.newsweek.com/woman-allegedly-breastfeeds-cat-delta-airlines-flight-1653656.

22 Napp Nazworth, "Conservative Protestant fertility has declined dramatically, study finds," CP Living, *Christian Post*, January 25, 2019, https://www.christianpost.com/news/conservative-protestant-fertility-has-declined-dramatically-study-finds.html.

23 Amanda Barroso, Kim Parker, and Jesse Bennet, "As Millennials Near 40, They're Approaching Family Life Differently Than Previous Generations," *Pew Research Center*, May 27, 2020, https://www.pewresearch.org/social-trends/2020/05/27/as-millennials-near-40-theyre-approaching-family-life-differently-than-previous-generations.

24 Randall O'Bannon, "62,502,904 Babies Have Been Killed in Abortions Since Roe v. Wade in 1973," National, *LifeNews.com*, January 18, 2021, https://www.lifenews.com/2021/01/18/62502904-babies-have-been-killed-in-abortions-since-roe-v-wade-in-1973.

25 "US States—Ranked by Population 2021," *World Population Review*, https://worldpopulationreview.com/states.

26 "Abortion Fact Sheet," *World Health Organization*, November 25, 2021, https://www.who.int/news-room/fact-sheets/detail/abortion.

27 Alexandra DeSanctis, "How Democrats purged 'safe, legal, rare' from the party," *Washington Post*, November 15, 2019, https://www.washingtonpost.com/outlook/how-democrats-purged-safe-legal-rare-from-the-party/2019/11/15/369af73c-01a4-11ea-8bab-0fc209e065a8_story.html.

28 Ibid.

29 Marie Solis, "Tulsi Gabbard's Stance on Abortion Is Stuck in the '90s," *Vice*, October 16, 2019, https://www.vice.com/en/article/43k5db/tulsi-gabbards-stance-on-abortion-is-stuck-in-the-90s.

30 Ibid.

31 Reproductive Health Act, https://legislation.nysenate.gov/pdf/bills/2019/A21.

32 Ibid.

33 Katie Reilly, "A New York Law Has Catapulted Later Abortion Back Into the Political Spotlight. Here's What the Legislation Actually Does," *Time,* February 1, 2019, https://time.com/5514644/later-abortion-new-york-law.

34 Alan Suderman, "Virginia abortion feud erupts; governor blasted for comments," *Associated Press,* January 30, 2019, https://apnews.com/article/health-ralph-northam-legislation-va-state-wire-womens-health-7f30ea0a5f1045aa82c130c9dece1ab8.

35 "WTOP's Ask the Governor with Virginia Gov. Ralph Northam-Jan. 30, 2019," WTOP News, https://www.youtube.com/watch?v=E6WD_3H0wKU/, pertinent portion begins at 38:45.

36 Kaia Hubbard, "A Guide to Abortion Laws by State," *U.S. News & World Report,* September 1, 2021, https://www.usnews.com/news/best-states/articles/a-guide-to-abortion-laws-by-state.

37 Adam Beam, "California plans to be abortion sanctuary if Roe overturned," *Associated Press,* December 8, 2021, https://apnews.com/article/abortion-california-sanctuary-625a118108bcda253196697c83548d5b.

38 Planned Parenthood, "By the Numbers," https://www.plannedparenthood.org/files/9313/9611/7194/Planned_Parenthood_By_The_Numbers.pdf.

39 Planned Parenthood, "Breakdown of Affiliate Medical Services," *2019–2020 Annual Report,* 35, https://www.plannedparenthood.org/uploads/filer_public/67/30/67305ea1-8da2-4cee-9191-19228c1d6f70/210219-annual-report-2019-2020-web-final.pdf.

40 Katherine Kortsmit, et al., "Abortion Surveillance—United States, 2019," https://www.cdc.gov/mmwr/volumes/70/ss/ss7009a1.htm.

41 Planned Parenthood, "Planned Parenthood Federation of America, Planned Parenthood Global, and Affiliate Financial Data," *2019– 2020 Annual Report*, 38, https://www.plannedparenthood.org/uploads/filer_ public/67/30/67305ea1-8da2-4cee-9191-19228c1d6f70/210219- annual-report-2019-2020-web-final.pdf.

42 Kate Smith, "Planned Parenthood launches $45 million investment in 2020 elections," *CBS News*, January 16, 2020, https://www.cbsnews. com/news/planned-parenthood-45-million-we-decide-2020- elections-investment-today.

43 "42 U.S. Code § 289g–2 - Prohibitions regarding human fetal tissue," https://www.law.cornell.edu/uscode/text/42/289g-2#:~:text=42%20 U.S.%20Code%20%C2%A7%20289g%E2%80%932%20%2D%20 Prohibitions%20regarding%20human%20fetal%20tissue,-U.S.%20 Code&text=It%20shall%20be%20unlawful%20for,the%20trans- fer%20affects%20interstate%20commerce.

44 "Planned Parenthood TX Abortion Apprentice Taught Partial-Birth Abortions to 'Strive For' Intact Heads," The Center for Medical Progress, https://www.youtube.com/watch?v=2tgez97aG74; "Planned Parenthood OC Changes Abortions to Harvest Intact Fetuses for Local Company's Sales," The Center for Medical Progress, https:// www.youtube.com/watch?v=Bwn0QBhy2TQ.

45 "Planned Parenthood Abortionist: 'Pay Attention to Who's in the Room' to Deal with Infants Born Alive," The Center for Medical Progress, https://www.youtube.com/watch?v=aeINzcwb3qU.

46 "Second Planned Parenthood Senior Executive Haggles over Baby Parts Prices, Changes Abortion Methods," The Center for Medical Progress, https://www.youtube.com/watch?v=MjCs_gvImyw.

47 Masha Gessen, quoted in "Homosexual activist says gay 'marriage' isn't about equality, it's about destroying marriage," *LifeSiteNews*, May 1, 2013, https://www.lifesitenews.com/news/homosexual-activist-says- gay-marriage-isnt-about-equality-its-about-destroy.

48 Hermann L. Strack and Paul Billerbeck, *A Commentary on the New Testament from the Talmud & Midrash*, ed. Jacob N. Cerone, trans. Andrew Bowden and Joseph Longarino (Bellingham, WA: Lexham, 2022), 338–56.

49 Ibid.

50 Demosthenes, "Against Neaera," *Orations*, trans. A. T. Murray, vol. 6, *Orations 50–59: Private Cases. In Neaeram*, Loeb Classical Library 351 (Cambridge, MA: Harvard University Press, 1939), https://www.loebclassics.com/view/demosthenes-orations_lix_theomnestus_apollodorus_neaera/1939/pb_LCL351.351.xml.

51 Bill C-4, https://www.parl.ca/DocumentViewer/en/44-1/bill/C-4/royal-assent.

52 "About," *Equip*, https://equipyourcommunity.org/about.

53 Pieter Valk, "What Are Celibate Partnerships? Are They Wise?," *Equip*, January 12, 2023, https://equipyourcommunity.org/celibate-partnerships.

54 Charles R. Erdman, *The Epistles of Paul to the Colossians and to Philemon* (Philadelphia: Westminster, 1966), 103.

55 Nancy Lehmann and Helen Sullinger, "The Document: Declaration of Feminism," 1971.

56 Ibid.

57 Sheila Cronan, "Marriage," in Anne Koedt, Ellen Levine, and Anita Rapone, eds., *Radical Feminism* (New York: Times Books, 1973), 219.

58 Luke Rosiak, "Loudoun County Schools Tried To Conceal Sexual Assault Against Daughter In Bathroom, Father Says," Investigation, *Daily Wire*, October 11, 2021, https://www.dailywire.com/news/loudoun-county-schools-tried-to-conceal-sexual-assault-against-daughter-in-bathroom-father-says.

59 James Queally and Anita Chabria, "Indecent exposure charges filed against trans woman over L.A. spa incident," California, *Los Angeles Times*, September 2, 2021, https://www.latimes.com/california/story/2021-09-02/indecent-exposure-charges-filed-trans-woman-spa.

60 Audrey Conklin and Michael Ruiz, "California trans child molester, 26, gets 2 years in juvenile facility thanks to progressive DA Gascon," Crime, *Fox News*, January 27, 2022, https://www.foxnews.com/us/transgender-ca-woman-molesting-sentenced.

61 Terry Thornton, "Governor Newsom signs Senate Bill 132," California Department of Corrections and Rehabilitation, September 29, 2020, https://www.cdcr.ca.gov/insidecdcr/2020/09/29/governor-newsom-signs-senate-bill-132-to-respect-gender-identity-during-incarceration.

62 Chris Field, "Women inmates condemn California for pro-trans law forcing them to be housed with, abused by men. State hands out condoms and pregnancy resources," News, *Blaze Media*, July 21, 2021, https://www.theblaze.com/news/california-women-inmates-housed-with-men-condoms.

63 Will Weissert, "Biden picks 1st transgender person for Senate-confirmed post," *Associated Press*, January 19, 2021, https://apnews.com/article/rachel-levine-health-secretary-4eee53439e9c2b4c27fcf4e7f572cb0e.

64 Department of Health and Human Services, "Statements by Officials of the U.S. Department of Health and Human Services Commemorating the First Openly Transgender Four-Star Officer and First Female Four-Star Admiral of the U.S. Public Health Service Commissioned Corps on October 19, 2021," News Release, October 19, 2021, https://www.hiv.gov/blog/statements-officials-us-department-health-and-human-services-commemorating-first-openly.

65 Ibid.

66 Ramona Tausz, "Biden's trans order undoes decades of feminist progress," Opinion, *New York Post*, January 22, 2021, https://nypost.com/2021/01/22/bidens-trans-order-undoes-decades-of-feminist-progress.

67 Ibid.

68 Ross Ibbetson and Britany Chain, "How Laurel Hubbard was a promising weightlifter as a teenage boy long before transitioning and aiming for Olympic glory as a woman," News, *Daily Mail*, August 2, 2021, https://www.dailymail.co.uk/news/article-9851639/How-Laurel-Hubbard-promising-weightlifter-teenage-boy-long-transitioning.html.

69 Adrian Seconi, "Otago University honours Hubbard," Sport, *Otago Daily Times*, October 2, 2021, https://www.odt.co.nz/sport/other-sport/otago-university-honours-hubbard.

70 Aleks Klosok and George Ramsay, "Weightlifter Laurel Hubbard becomes first out transgender woman to compete at the Olympics, fails to register a lift," Sports, *CNN*, August 2, 2021, https://www.cnn.com/2021/08/02/sport/laurel-hubbard-olympics-weightlifting-spt-intl/index.html.

71 Tat Bellamy-Walker, "Trans swimmer Lia Thomas wins 4 races at Ivy championships, heads to NCAA finals," Out News, *NBC News*, February 22, 2022, https://www.nbcnews.com/nbc-out/out-news/trans-swimmer-lia-thomas-wins-4-races-ivy-championships-heads-ncaa-fin-rcna17227.

72 Patrick Reilly, "Teammates say they are uncomfortable changing in locker room with trans UPenn swimmer Lia Thomas," Sports, *New York Post*, January 27, 2022, https://nypost.com/2022/01/27/teammates-are-uneasy-changing-in-locker-room-with-trans-upenn-swimmer-lia-thomas.

73 Yaron Steinbuch, "Transgender swimmer Lia Thomas is 'destroying' sport, official says," Sports, *New York Post*, December 28, 2021, https://nypost.com/2021/12/28/official-transgender-swimmer-lia-thomas-is-destroying-the-sport.

74 Ibid.

75 Jon Johnson, "What to know about toxic masculinity," *Medical News Today*, June 22, 2020, https://www.medicalnewstoday.com/articles/toxic-masculinity.

76 Ibid.

77 Stephanie Pappas, "APA issues first-ever guidelines for practice with
   men and boys," *American Psychological Association* 50, no. 1 (2019):
   34,
   https://www.apa.org/monitor/2019/01/ce-corner.
78 Ibid.
79 Ibid.
80 Ben Shapiro, "The Attack on Masculinity," *The Ben Shapiro Show*,
   Episode 1139, aired November 17, 2020,
   https://www.youtube.com/watch?v=3pUlUey50Gg.
81 Ibid.
82 Ibid.
83 William Hendrikson, *Exposition of the Pastoral Epistles* (Grand
   Rapids: Baker, 1981), 122.
84 Richard Baxter, *The Reformed Pastor* (Edinburgh: Banner of Truth,
   1979), 63.
85 Geoffery B. Wilson, *The Pastoral Epistles* (Edinburgh: Banner of
   Truth, 1982), 50.

# INDEX OF SCRIPTURE

**Genesis**

| | |
|---|---|
| 1:26 | 138 |
| 1:27 | 138 |
| 1:27–28 | 38, 147 |
| 1:28 | 106, 168 |
| 2:18 | 44, 121, 178 |
| 2:21–24 | 121 |
| 2:21–25 | 45 |
| 2:24 | 164 |
| 3 | 184 |
| 3:16 | 39, 167, 168, 177 |
| 3:20 | 39 |
| 4 | 39 |
| 4:1–16 | 39 |
| 4:7 | 168 |
| 4:10 | 141 |
| 4:19–24 | 39 |
| 5:1 | 111 |
| 6:1–7 | 39 |
| 9:6 | 139 |
| 11:1–9 | 40 |
| 16:2–4 | 31 |
| 17:20 | 31 |
| 18:11–14 | 123 |
| 29:31–35 | 45, 123 |

**Exodus**

| | |
|---|---|
| 20:5 | xiii, xiv, 3 |
| 20:12 | 49, 50 |
| 20:13 | 140 |
| 20:17 | 158 |
| 21:22–25 | 140 |
| 34:7 | 4, 86 |

**Leviticus**

| | |
|---|---|
| 10:9 | 200 |
| 18:21 | 24 |

**Numbers**

| | |
|---|---|
| 14:18 | xiii, 4 |

**Deuteronomy**

| | |
|---|---|
| 4:9 | 70, 93 |
| 4:9–10 | 69 |
| 4:24–28 | 10 |
| 4:40 | 69 |
| 5 | 4 |
| 5:6–9 | 5 |
| 5:9 | 4 |
| 5:9–10 | 58 |
| 5:10 | 5 |
| 6 | 5, 49, 87 |
| 6:1–2 | 6 |
| 6:3 | 6, 71 |
| 6:4–6 | 6 |
| 6:4–9 | 68, 86 |
| 6:5 | 71 |
| 6:6 | 71 |
| 6:7 | 7, 8, 69, 70, 71 |
| 6:8–9 | 7, 72 |
| 6:9 | 8 |
| 6:10–11 | 8 |
| 6:10–12 | 72 |
| 6:12–15 | 9 |
| 6:18 | 71 |
| 7:12–13 | 46, 122 |
| 8:18 | 72 |
| 11:18–19 | 68 |
| 12:8 | 20 |
| 12:19–31 | 21 |
| 12:28 | 21 |
| 12:31 | 21 |
| 18:9–10 | 24 |
| 24:1 | 148 |

**Judges**

| | |
|---|---|
| 2:6–8 | 10 |
| 2:7 | 11 |
| 2:8 | 11 |
| 2:10 | 10, 11 |
| 2:11–12 | 12 |
| 2:13 | 12, 19 |
| 2:14–15 | 19 |
| 2:16–17 | 19 |
| 21:25 | 20, 178 |

**Ruth**

| | |
|---|---|
| 4:13 | 31, 123 |
| 4:14–15 | 123 |

**1 Samuel**

| | |
|---|---|
| 1:19–20 | 31 |
| 15:23 | 61 |

**2 Samuel**

| | |
|---|---|
| 4:11 | 141 |
| 12 | 41 |
| 12:20–23 | 42 |
| 18 | 42 |

**1 Kings**

| | |
|---|---|
| 11:7 | 23 |

**2 Kings**

| | |
|---|---|
| 17:17 | 24 |
| 23:13 | 23 |

**Job**

| | |
|---|---|
| 9:25–26 | 119 |
| 14:1–2 | 119 |

Psalms

| | |
|---|---|
| 1 | 94 |
| 22:9 | 31 |
| 51:5 | 33, 58 |
| 58:3 | 33, 78 |
| 73:25–28 | 115 |
| 78:6–7 | 70 |
| 82:3–4 | 139 |
| 90:12 | 120 |
| 113:9 | 46, 122 |
| 115:14–15 | 46 |
| 127:3 | 30, 115 |
| 127:3–5 | 46, 122 |
| 127:4–5 | 18 |
| 128 | 47, 122 |
| 139 | 30 |
| 139:1–3 | 31 |
| 139:13 | 136 |
| 139:13–17 | 31 |
| 139:14 | 137 |
| 139:15 | 137 |
| 139:16 | 137 |

Proverbs

| | |
|---|---|
| 1:1–7 | 74 |
| 1:7 | 76 |
| 1:8 | 60, 74 |
| 1:10 | 95 |
| 1:11–19 | 95 |
| 2:1 | 75 |
| 2:11–15 | 95 |
| 2:16 | 97 |
| 3 | 100 |
| 3:1 | 75 |
| 3:3 | 93 |
| 3:5–6 | 120 |
| 3:13–18 | 91 |
| 4 | 51 |
| 4:1 | 75 |
| 4:1–4 | 51 |
| 4:5 | 91 |
| 4:6–9 | 92 |
| 4:10 | 51 |
| 4:10–12 | 92 |
| 4:10–18 | 96 |
| 4:11–18 | 52 |
| 4:23 | 87, 93 |
| 4:24 | 78, 93 |
| 5:3–8 | 97 |
| 5:12–14 | 98 |
| 5:21–23 | 97 |
| 6 | 100 |
| 6:12 | 78 |
| 6:16–19 | 78 |
| 6:17 | 140 |
| 6:20–23 | 98 |
| 6:24–29 | 99 |
| 6:32–33 | 99 |
| 7:22 | 99 |
| 7:24 | 99 |
| 8:36 | 75 |
| 9:10 | 76 |
| 10:1 | 48 |
| 10:11 | 78 |

| | |
|---|---|
| 10:13 | 78 |
| 10:14 | 78 |
| 10:18 | 78 |
| 10:19–21 | 78 |
| 10:31 | 78 |
| 10:32 | 78 |
| 12:15 | 75 |
| 13:5 | 79 |
| 13:22 | 85 |
| 13:24 | 48 |
| 16:14 | 162 |
| 17:7 | 79 |
| 18:24 | 96 |
| 19:14 | 162 |
| 19:18 | 48 |
| 20:1 | 200 |
| 22:6 | xii, 52, 100 |
| 22:15 | 49, 66, 75 |
| 23:7 | 93 |
| 23:13–14 | 49, 67 |
| 23:23 | 91 |
| 26:28 | 79 |
| 27:1 | 119 |
| 29:12 | 79 |
| 29:15 | 87 |
| 29:17 | 48 |
| 31:4–5 | 200 |
| 31:6 | 200 |

Ecclesiastes

| | |
|---|---|
| 2:1–11 | 113 |
| 5:10 | 116 |
| 12:13–14 | 114 |

Isaiah

| | |
|---|---|
| 3 | 182 |
| 3:12 | 180 |
| 3:16 | 178 |
| 3:17–24 | 179 |
| 3:25 | 179 |
| 3:26 | 180 |
| 8:18 | 18 |

Jeremiah

| | |
|---|---|
| 5 | 79 |
| 5:3 | 80 |
| 5:4–5 | 80 |
| 5:5 | 81 |
| 5:7 | 81 |
| 7:31 | 25 |
| 31:29 | 4 |
| 32:17–18 | 4 |
| 32:18 | xiv |

Ezekiel

| | |
|---|---|
| 16:20–21 | 25 |
| 16:21 | 18 |
| 16:36–38 | 25, 133 |
| 18:20 | xiv |
| 20:30–31 | 26, 134 |
| 23:37 | 26 |
| 23:39 | 26 |
| 33:11 | 160 |

Jonah

| | |
|---|---|
| 4:11 | 18, 33 |

Matthew

| | |
|---|---|
| 5:27–28 | 158 |
| 5:28 | 199 |
| 5:29–30 | 158 |
| 5:31–32 | 148 |
| 6:19–21 | 118 |
| 6:24 | 117 |
| 10:16 | 202 |
| 12:33–35 | 94 |
| 19 | 29 |
| 19:6 | 121 |
| 19:13–14 | 18 |
| 19:14 | 133 |
| 22:38 | 71 |
| 26:52 | 139 |

Mark

| | |
|---|---|
| 7:20 | 87 |
| 7:20–23 | 88 |
| 9:36 | 31 |
| 10 | 29 |
| 10:13 | 32 |
| 10:13–16 | 29 |
| 10:14 | 32 |
| 10:16 | 31 |
| 12:29–31 | 89 |
| 14:38 | 93 |

Luke

| | |
|---|---|
| 1:41 | 140 |
| 1:44 | 140 |
| 2:12 | 140 |
| 2:16 | 140 |
| 2:52 | 90 |
| 12 | 119 |
| 12:4–5 | 76 |
| 12:6 | 77 |
| 12:7 | 77 |
| 12:8 | 77 |
| 12:15–21 | 116 |
| 14:12–14 | 202 |
| 17:2 | 34 |
| 18 | 29 |
| 18:15 | 32 |

John

| | |
|---|---|
| 1:3 | 136 |
| 3:3 | 88 |
| 3:7 | 88 |
| 14:6 | 71, 79 |
| 15:18–19 | 208 |
| 15:18–20 | 147 |
| 17:17 | 79 |

Acts

| | |
|---|---|
| 7:43 | 23 |
| 17:22–25 | 135 |
| 17:26 | 136 |
| 17:28 | 136 |
| 20:33 | 205 |

**Romans**
| | |
|---|---|
| 1 | 151, 152, 155 |
| 1:16 | 84 |
| 1:18–20 | 110 |
| 1:21–23 | 111 |
| 1:24 | 151, 152 |
| 1:25 | 111 |
| 1:26–27 | 152 |
| 1:26–32 | 152 |
| 2:14–15 | 92 |
| 3:10 | 33, 89 |
| 3:23 | 33, 88 |
| 8:1 | 35 |
| 11:36 | 115 |
| 12:1–2 | 158 |
| 12:2 | 93 |
| 12:18 | 205 |

**1 Corinthians**
| | |
|---|---|
| 1:30 | 75 |
| 2:16 | 76 |
| 3:19 | 43 |
| 6:9 | 157 |
| 6:9–10 | 159 |
| 6:11 | 159 |
| 6:18 | 99 |
| 7:23 | 114 |
| 9:24–27 | 198 |
| 10:31 | 114 |
| 11:6 | 176 |
| 13:5 | 204 |
| 14:33 | 177 |
| 14:34 | 177 |
| 14:34–35 | 177 |
| 14:35 | 176 |
| 15:9 | 207 |

**2 Corinthians**
| | |
|---|---|
| 5:11 | 76 |
| 5:17 | 199 |
| 5:21 | 160 |
| 7:1 | 159 |
| 10:3–5 | 17 |
| 10:4 | 83 |

**Ephesians**
| | |
|---|---|
| 2:8–9 | 185 |
| 2:10 | 114 |
| 4:13 | 196 |
| 4:14 | 196 |
| 4:22–23 | 159 |
| 5 | 45, 121 |
| 5:18 | 65 |
| 5:22 | 161 |
| 5:22–24 | 160 |
| 5:23 | 161 |
| 5:25 | 162 |
| 5:26–27 | 163 |
| 5:28–29 | 163 |
| 5:31 | 164 |
| 6 | 50 |
| 6:1 | 50, 90, 98 |
| 6:1–2 | 59 |
| 6:2–3 | 50 |

| | |
|---|---|
| 6:4 | viii, 34, 50, 54, 59, 60, 66, 67, 87 |
| 6:12 | 83 |

**Philippians**
| | |
|---|---|
| 3:14 | 196 |
| 4:8 | 201 |

**Colossians**
| | |
|---|---|
| 2:3 | 76 |
| 3:2 | 159 |
| 3:20 | 90, 98 |
| 3:21 | 48, 61 |

**1 Thessalonians**
| | |
|---|---|
| 5:6 | 14 |

**1 Timothy**
| | |
|---|---|
| 1:13 | 141 |
| 1:15 | 207 |
| 2:9 | 182 |
| 2:10 | 182 |
| 2:11–12 | 184 |
| 2:13–14 | 184 |
| 2:15 | 185, 187 |
| 3 | 197 |
| 3:2 | 197, 198, 200, 201, 203 |
| 3:2–7 | 197 |
| 3:3 | 203, 204, 205 |
| 3:4–5 | 205 |
| 3:5 | 182 |
| 3:6 | 206, 207 |
| 3:7 | 207 |
| 3:15 | 182 |
| 5:23 | 200 |
| 6:6–10 | 205 |
| 6:7 | 117 |
| 6:8 | 117 |
| 6:9–10 | 117 |
| 6:17 | 115 |

**2 Timothy**
| | |
|---|---|
| 1:5 | 73 |
| 2:13 | 79 |
| 2:24 | 204 |
| 3:15 | 73 |
| 3:16 | 74, 196 |
| 3:17 | 196 |

**Titus**
| | |
|---|---|
| 1:2 | 79 |
| 1:11 | 176 |
| 2:3–5 | 181 |
| 2:5 | 181 |
| 2:10 | 182 |
| 2:11–12 | 183 |

**Hebrews**
| | |
|---|---|
| 2:13 | 18 |
| 10:31 | 34, 76, 92 |
| 11:23 | 59 |
| 12 | 66 |
| 12:6 | 66 |
| 12:6–7 | 48 |

| | |
|---|---|
| 12:10 | 48 |
| 12:29 | 34 |
| 13:2 | 202 |

**James**
| | |
|---|---|
| 1:14–15 | 97 |
| 1:27 | 139 |
| 3:9 | 138 |
| 4:13–15 | 119 |

**1 Peter**
| | |
|---|---|
| 3:1–2 | 183 |
| 3:3–4 | 183 |
| 3:5–6 | 184 |
| 3:7 | 44, 121 |

**1 John**
| | |
|---|---|
| 3:13 | 73 |
| 5:19 | 144 |

**Jude**
| | |
|---|---|
| 3 | 204 |

JOHN MACARTHUR PUBLISHING GROUP
LOS ANGELES, CALIFORNIA